I was a Minister in the Nation of Islam

I was a Minister in the Nation of Islam

Now I'm a Minister for Christ

Alexis Johnson

Pleasant Word
A Division of WinePress Group

Pleasant Word (a division of WinePress Publishing, PO Box 428, Enumclaw, WA 98022) functions only as book publisher. As such, the ultimate design, content, editorial accuracy, and views expressed or implied in this work are those of the author.

ISBN 13: 978-1-4141-1341-8
ISBN 10: 1-4141-1341-2
Library of Congress Catalog Card Number: 2008909660

I dedicate this book to my four adult children: Lorraine, Sasheena, Bishara, and Khalif. I raised all of them to be Muslims in the Nation of Islam and then Orthodox Islam. Sasheena, Bishara, and Khalif have come to accept Jesus Christ as their personal Lord and Savior.

I also dedicate this book to my twin sister, Amelia, who led me to the Lord; to my late Pastor David E. Alston and his wife Pastor Lessie Alston; and to my present pastor Dr. Joseph Okpanachi—my spiritual mentors.

Special Thanks

To my mother, Dora Lee Johnson-McClendon. Thank you for your prayers. I am alive because of them.

Special thanks to Deborah Elmore-Harrell, who proofread the early part of my writing. Special thanks to the Reverend Kathleen Schwartzer and Thomas Gadson Sr. for your help.

Also, thanks to Margaret Ann Postell for your help in making sure this book came into publication.

Special thanks to my friends Arthur and Ceriene Lofton for your prayers and words of encouragement.

A big thank you to Renee Michelle Moreau for editing and proofreading the manuscript and organizing the sections and chapters.

Contents

Foreword

MY BACKGROUND IN Folk Islam gives me a great appreciation for this book. Alexis Johnson lucidly and concisely speaks to several often neglected reasons why many African American young men are converting to the Nation of Islam at an alarming rate. African American men are attracted to Islam because they long for structure and order in their lives. The Christian church offers structure and order in the form of accountability, but this is not readily seen. The process of Johnson's conversion to the Nation of Islam is quite interesting and opens up an avenue for dialogue on how the church can best respond to those with proclivity toward the message of the NOI. Johnson's experience is indeed an enlightening guide! This is a must read book. I heartily recommend it!

—Dr. Joseph Okpanachi

Introduction

THERE IS MUCH to learn from what Alexis Johnson has seen and heard.

His journey began when his family moved from the segregated south to Red Bank, New Jersey, in the 1940s. After some bitter experiences as a young boy, it was clear he had been groomed to choose the path of least resistance in life. Disillusioned by the Christian church and later saved by the message of Islam, Alexis found no resolution to the conflict of his identity as a black man in the real world.

He writes his story knowing there are many who will relate. Though his particular journey brought him under the tutelage of both Elijah Muhammad and the Minister Louis Farrakhan, not one seeker goes unaffected by the dizzying warfare between politics, power, and the salvation of souls. Keeping in touch with the history and issues of the black American experience, this book offers unique and authentic insights into the reality of this struggle and can help those in confusion to discern the *more excellent way.*

Alexis' journey has obviously come full-circle. He is now ministering to those whose hearts he knows best, and it has been my privilege to witness him tell his story.

—Renee Michelle Moreau

CHAPTER ONE

My Black Experience

NIGGER, DO YOU see this blackjack? I am going to teach you a lesson." Standing before me were two huge white men, terrorizing me, a skinny sixteen-year-old black boy. It was 1966 and we were in the juvenile section on the third floor of the old Monmouth County Jail in Freehold, New Jersey.

"Take off your clothes," they said to me. But I refused. I could only think about being sexually molested by a white man as a little boy. After arguments and threats, I decided to comply except for my underwear. They took me downstairs and threw me into a ten-by-ten foot metal box called "the hole," which was on the first floor of the jail. It was cold and pitch black, except for a little light that shone through a tiny peephole. Three times a day, bread, soup, and water were shoved through a slot in the door. I spent most of my time lying on the cold, hard, concrete floor, while reflecting on my life.

My parents, Pernell Johnson Sr. and Dora Lee Johnson-McClendon, were from Franklinton, North Carolina.

We colored people or Negroes (as we were called) knew where we stood: segregation was the law. Negroes went to segregated schools and lived in segregated neighborhoods with colored-only water fountains. Negroes could not eat at the same counter in a restaurant with white people. We had to sit at the back of a bus, and if a white person needed a seat, we had to give up ours.

My parents decided to move to Red Bank in the early 1940s.[†] Like many of the Negroes who moved north, they expected a different kind of life. Moving up north was considered moving to a place of better opportunity where we would be treated fairly, but we met the same old discrimination.

For instance, my parents filled out an application to rent an apartment on the east side of town. They were denied and never given a reason. There were times when they would go into a restaurant and would have to wait until all the white people were served, and they were expected not to complain. They had heard that the KKK had a presence in Red Bank. Many members of the organization were business owners, but it was hard to tell members from those who were simply afraid of attracting the Klan's attention.[1‡]

My father had a very difficult time finding work. He was a cook by trade and was satisfied with making ten dollars a week, wanting only to support his family. He soon became disillusioned by the false promises of the north and began to drink alcohol, another illusion of escape.

Though he was an alcoholic, he was still a good provider. At times, under the influence of alcohol, he would be physically abusive, especially towards my mother. I remember the police coming to our home several times, taking my father out in handcuffs. In spite of all the turmoil, I remember my mother always displayed good Christian conduct. As a child, I never saw her drink alcohol nor heard her use profanity.

I was raised as a Christian in the Salvation Army, which at the time was a predominantly white congregation located on the east side of town. We were one of two black families who attended. The commanding officers were Captains Mr. and Mrs. Clay, both pastors and a white couple, who were very loving and kind. My mother became a member in 1955 when I was five years old. I had seven brothers and three sisters and we all attended church with my mother. I still have my certificate of promotion from Primary 1 Class to Primary 2 Class, signed by Mrs. Clay and dated 1956. It was something I could call my own! However, in spite of our involvement and the size of the Johnson footprint in that congregation, my father never became a member. I don't recall any programs within the church that addressed the problem of alcoholism, nor whether there were any such programs within the community. After all, this was the 1950s. At church as at home, he was, for all practical purposes, absent.

RED BANK, N. J., THURSDAY, JULY 6, 1961

MUSICAL GROUP — This musical group of Red Bank area Salvation Army players left yesterday for a 10-day sojourn at Star Lake Camp, Bloomington, where Salvation Army band groups vacation. Edward Conway, chairman of the Salvation Army Camp Fund, estimates that about 150 young people from northeastern Monmouth County will take part in the camping program. Directing it is Al Swenarton, Ocean Grove, bandmaster of the Army's Asbury Park corps. Shown here, left to right, are Robert Folkenburt, Rumson; Thomas Johnson, Lessie Johnson, Edward Johnson and Alonis Johnson, Red Bank; Carol McManus, West Keansburg; Pamala Schmidt, Rumson; Timothy Johnson, Red Bank; Diane McManus, West Keansburg, and Frank Lloyd, Red Bank.

July 6, 1961

My mother took us to church every Sunday. There we learned all the Bible stories in Sunday school. We were taught that Jesus died for our sins. I can even remember asking Jesus to come into my heart, yet I never knew him as my personal savior. I liked going to church because it was a fun place. It gave me opportunities other kids in my community did not have, such as a free pass to summer camp each year, free church dinners (for a family of ten, that meant a lot), and even music lessons. I learned to play the trombone and would participate during Sunday worship.

At Christmas time I would play beside the red kettle collection in front of the market, which always encouraged people to be generous. The Salvation Army would give the children a small stipend for such services. My peers would make fun of me for spending my time helping the church. I guess I stood out. However, as I grew older, I went to church mostly just for something to do. Many times staying involved was an escape from the turbulence at home. Consequently, the conflict between my home life and the life I heard preached about left me very confused.

The congregation was loving and kind. Our large family had great needs, and the church was very helpful to our family. Each year I looked forward to going to Christian camp. But around the age of ten I began to experience racial name-calling and one summer I was sexually abused by a camp counselor, who happened to be white. I became very angry and defensive and stopped trusting people in authority. Subconsciously, I also began to hate white people.

Unresolved resentment would ebb and flow inside me, and gradually I began to rebel, but I never really understood why. I lived on the west side of the railroad tracks that separated the two sides of town, and ninety-five percent of the people were black. On the east side of the tracks, ninety-five percent of the people were white.

The old saying "he's from the wrong side of the tracks" seemed like it applied to me. I remember incidents of racism and name-calling both in my community and school, which were divided, though not officially segregated. Those railroad tracks stood as a powerful metaphor of the racial divide that still persists. Like some metaphysical monument, they were a constant reminder of the racially-charged social code that was constantly running in the thoughts of the families who lived there. Just as one can get used to the noise of a train when living under its influence day after day, the people of Red Bank were used to the noise of hatred and racism that had been generated by the presence of the Klan.

When I was in the sixth grade, my teacher asked all of the students what they wanted to be when they grew up. I was so excited that I could not wait until she asked me.

"Alexis" she finally said, "what do you want to be when you grow up? What is your dream?"

"I want to be an engineer!"

"An engineer? You can't be an engineer. You're not smart enough. Forget about that dream," she said with a wave of her hand.

From that day forward I stopped taking my education seriously. I just stopped trying. At the end of that school year my report card read, "Failed. Must repeat the sixth grade." The following years were a blur of struggling relationships and depression.

One day when I was sixteen, four white boys jumped me from behind in the school yard at Red Bank High School. While they were kicking me and stomping me, I remember my teacher stood by watching. Since the teacher did not attempt to stop them, I pulled out a straight-edged razor that I carried in my pocket for protection. The four boys began to run and I chased them. Immediately I heard the teacher yelling for someone to call the police. Shortly after the police arrived, I was handcuffed and thrown into a police car. At the police headquarters I was charged with assault and battery, carrying a concealed weapon, and threatening to do bodily harm. That's how I wound up at the juvenile section of the county jail.

I was locked up in a cell for twenty-three hours a day with no visitation rights, not even from my parents. We were given no Bibles, books, or materials of any kind to read. However, there was a black and white television set with three channels that sat just outside of the cell block. Most of us could not see the television where it was positioned, but we could hear it. It was kind of surreal to watch the white men sitting freely under the influence of the black and white set, while the mostly black inmates could hear, but not quite perceive, what was going on. Only later did I come to understand the irony of it.

After weeks of being locked up with no sunlight or fresh air, I became angry and frustrated. At my wit's end, I began to protest loudly and incited other inmates to do the same. Because of that, the officers took our mattresses away. For seven days we slept on bedsprings or cold concrete. I had enough, so I stuffed the toilet with paper, encouraging others to join in the "protest." Consequently, the whole cellblock flooded.

An officer came in and said, "I won't let you out until you tell me who started this." No one would talk, so he added, "You niggers can clean this up and you all lose your one hour of privilege. You're now on a twenty-four hour lock down."

I could not let the others suffer for what I had started, so I confessed. The other inmates were then led out of their cells so they could be cleaned, while I was taken to the warden's office, threatened, and thrown in the "hole" for six days. After being released, I was taken back to my cell and placed on twenty-four hour lock down with no mattress.

The day finally came for my court appointment. I was told by the warden (to torment me, I suppose) that I would most likely be locked up until my eighteenth birthday. On the day of the court hearing, my family and many others came to support me. The captain from the Salvation Army also came to speak to the judge on my behalf. He shared that I was an active member of the local band and had no prior record or problems with the courts. The judge coolly stated that the charges against me were very serious and he would have to send me away. The parents of the boys who had jumped me also demanded that I be locked up. When it was time for the judge to make his decision, I looked over at the white boys as they laughed.

Suddenly one of the boys jumped up and asked the judge for permission to speak to him before he made his decision. The judge took him into his chambers, while I sat with sweat running down my face. The ten minutes or so they conferred seemed like hours. Finally, they came out and I looked at the boy, then the judge, to see if I could catch a clue as to what had been said. I was very surprised when the judge told everyone in the courtroom what had been shared privately. The parents and the other three boys were surprised too. The truth had come out.

The boy confessed that they had provoked the fight, not me. My family and I were then called into the judge's chambers. He wanted to address the fact that I had been carrying a weapon the day of the attack and had attempted to use it. Thankfully, my two aunts, who had come from New York to support me, suggested that the court allow them to take me back with them. The judge explained that if I left the state of New Jersey I could not return until I reached the age of eighteen. Then I would no longer be a juvenile, and he never wanted to see me again in his courtroom. That was 1967. I was seventeen and very much relieved to be out of jail.

The Path of Least Resistance

I moved with my two aunts to East Elmhurst Queens, New York, but much like my parents' move north, it was like going from the frying pan into the fire. There was an area on Northern Boulevard nicknamed "Vietnam" because it was like a war zone. Shootings were a regular occurrence because of the heavy traffic of drugs. Nevertheless, I had to think about starting a new life in these surroundings.

Initially, I tried to enroll in school but I didn't have the self-esteem or enough faith in the system to persevere, so I gave up. I started hanging out on the street and with the wrong people. Before long, I was caught up in the drug culture.

I always enjoyed the feeling I got from dressing nice and having money in my pocket, but I could not find a job because I was too young and had no skills. When I say I was too young, I mean that I was not perceived as responsible, and no skills meant I was perceived as too much trouble to teach. Quite a few people my age and of my color made easy money selling drugs. That's how most of the boys in East Elmhurst, a predominantly black neighborhood, got by in those days.

One day a major drug dealer offered me a job as one of his runners. A runner was one who would sell drugs for the person who bought the drugs wholesale. The first time I went out as a runner, the dealer gave me thirty bags (called bundles) of heroin. They sold for $3.00 per bag on the street. I was surprised at how easily and quickly they sold. I informed my aunts that I did not want to go to school, that I had a job and would be glad to pay them rent. They thought I had a real job. It wasn't long before I had a pocket full of money and plenty of women. I began to carry a gun because there was always someone who was trying to take me off (rob me of my money and drugs). I also had to look out for the police because they were known to stop runners and take our stash. They were the biggest takeoff artists.

I remember leaving the Bedford Stuyvesant section of Brooklyn about 2:00 A.M. one morning. I had about ten nickel (five dollar) bags of marijuana on me. Suddenly I heard police sirens and noticed a car pulling over. Two uniformed police officers jumped out, one black and one white. They threw me on the ground and said they had stopped me because I had just robbed someone. I told them that wasn't true and I could prove where I had just come from. When they searched me, they found the bags of marijuana. They looked at the marijuana and said, "We're going to be nice and let you go." They took my drugs and left. I don't know if they were being nice to me or not. Many young men my age were being shot and killed because of drugs.

By this time, I was known in the community for running many bundles, which meant I carried a lot of cash. Of course, most of it belonged to the person for whom I was selling the drugs. I was a target for the older guys to try to take me off, but I would run and they knew that I carried a gun and would not hesitate to use it.

One day on Northern Boulevard, my luck ran out. Two guys came from behind, put a gun to my head, and told me not to turn around. "Give me the drugs and money, or die," they said. What could I do? I knew that I could not go back to the person I worked for without the stash. I had seen him beat or kill runners because they did not return his money or unsold drugs.

I said to myself, "I am not going to allow anyone to beat me, and I am certainly not ready to die." I gave up the stash and took a few of my boys to another part of New York. No one knew us, so we robbed a few drug dealers to pay off my boss.

I had so much money from robbing other drug dealers that I bought my own supply of heroin and began to work for myself. Soon, I started snorting heroin up my nose. After a while I got tired of that and started shooting heroin into my veins. Before I knew what hit me, I was shooting two to three bags of heroin per day. I was also giving heroin away to some of my friends who promised to pay me later, but of course they never did. My money supply ran low as I turned from drug dealer to user. In fact, twice I overdosed on heroin.

One day my friends and I went up town to Harlem to coop (to buy) some heroin. The word on the street was that the best dope was called "red label." It was the most potent. People were accidentally overdosing on it all over New York. We decided we needed to get some.

After scoring and going back to my friend's house in Queens, I went straight to the bathroom, pulled out my works (a syringe and a bottle cap), opened the two small glossy bags of heroin, poured the contents in the bottle cap, and started cooking the dope. I took off my belt and tied it around by arm above the elbow. I was getting excited. I picked up my syringe and began drawing the heroin from the bottle. "Ah," I said to myself. I had found a strong vein just waiting to be penetrated with the syringe. I pushed the needle into my vein and watched as the blood began to ooze out into the syringe.

Later on I heard voices screaming, "Al, wake up. Wake up!" One of the guys who was with me had placed ice under my testicles and was pouring cold water all over my face.

"What happened?" I asked. Then I realized I had overdosed. I never went to the hospital and no one would take me. Going to the hospital was reserved for the dead.

Somehow I knew that life was meant to be more than this. So I began to go to church with my two aunts. Deep inside I wanted to hear something that could help my life. But all they talked about was heaven and what it was going to be like when we died. I often stared at the picture of the white, blue-eyed Jesus on the center wall of the church. "What about now? Is there a better life for me *now*?" I said to myself. It seemed like the church had nothing to offer me. There were no role models my age, nor was there anyone who could offer me any concrete help in finding a place to start. The church was asleep—irresponsive to the culture and irrelevant to me.

A New Identity

The Muslims of The Nation of Islam (NOI) were making themselves visible on the streets of East Elmhurst, Queens, with a black version of social justice, pushing black nation building, entrepreneurship, and a taste of heaven on earth. I did not know anything about NOI, so I decided to purchase a copy the *Autobiography of Malcolm X.*

I remember one time entering an NOI restaurant called Shabazz (translated "from the lost tribe") on 102nd Street and Northern Boulevard in Queens around 1967, carrying my copy of the book. One of the Muslim brothers came up to me and said, "Brother, you are welcome in here, but not with that book. Please leave it outside, then you can come back." I had no idea why he said that. It was not until I had read the book that I realized that the Muslims of the Nation of Islam saw Malcolm X as a traitor and hated him. Malcolm X had heard rumors as far back as 1955 that

Elijah Muhammad, the head of the NOI at the time, had sexual relationships with teenage girls. He mentioned in his book that it was reported over radio and television some time around about 1963 that the sixty-seven-year-old leader of the Black Muslim movement faced paternity suits from two former secretaries, who charged that he had fathered their four children. Malcolm said he simply refused to accept anything as grotesque as adultery regarding Elijah Muhammad.

Malcolm X had searched the Bible and Quran for rationalization for such acts. In April of 1963, he flew to Elijah Muhammad's home in Phoenix, Arizona, to inquire firsthand about the statements of adultery. By the time he detailed the meeting in his book, he had found a way to justify such abuses.

> "Well, son," Mr. Muhammad said, "what is on your mind?" I told Mr. Muhammad what was being said. And without waiting for any response from him, I said that with his son Wallace's help I had found in the Quran and the Bible that which might be taught to Muslims—if it became necessary—as the fulfillment of prophecy.
>
> "Son, I'm not surprised," Elijah Muhammad said. "You always have had such a good understanding of prophecy and spiritual things. You recognize that's what all of this is: prophecy." "I'm David," he said. "When you read about how David took another man's wife, I'm that David. You read about Noah, who got drunk—that's me. You read about Lot who went and lay up with his own daughters. I have to fulfill all of those things."[2]

Malcolm X was born Malcolm Little in 1925, the son of Reverend Earl Little, a Baptist preacher. He experienced racism firsthand at the hands of the Ku Klux Klan and had once lived in the East Elmhurst section of Queens, New York, not far from where I lived. It turned out that my two aunts had known his wife, Betty Shabazz, years before I had come to live with them as a teenager. Malcolm X, who was a budding reformer of the movement, was assassinated on February 21, 1965. It is believed, but not proven, that the members of the Nation of Islam are responsible for his death. I was fascinated but not persuaded either way in my opinion of the organization.

Whenever I saw Muslims on the streets, I noticed how clean they looked, how the women dressed, and how well respected they were. I saw many former drug dealers and drug addicts now clean and running legitimate businesses. They had their own barbershops, bakeries, restaurants, clothing stores, dry cleaning stores, and bookstores in the community. This was the antithesis of the white community I had grown up in back in New Jersey, but this was no small town movement.

On 116th Street and Lennox Avenue in New York City, there was a Muslim school, K-12th grade. While studying with the organization in 1973, I learned that on the national level, the NOI owned 35,000 acres of farmland in the states of Georgia, Michigan, and Alabama where they grew and produced their own food. In the city of Chicago, they had their own supermarket, clothing factory, and newspaper plant where the paper *Muhammad Speaks* was printed. They owned a fleet of tractor-trailer trucks and shipped the newspapers all over America. They also built homes and apartment buildings exclusively for NOI members in Chicago. There was employment for their members all over the country.

I was impressed with this group of people. To be exposed to people of color who were successfully building their own communities, with the help of this organization, gave me hope for my own future, which I had not seen modeled anywhere else. However, I neglected to ask myself what it meant to build a separate black nation within the United States. I didn't realize they were demanding the United States pay restitution for slavery by providing the black races with their own territory. They thought this would make everything right between the races (this is a keynote in NOI ideology to this day). What I did ask myself was, "What are the churches doing for the black man?" I began to seriously doubt the Christian church.

One day I went to a Muslim-owned dry cleaners in the East Elmhurst section of Queens to drop off some clothes. There was a Muslim sister at the counter and she said to me, "Brother, how old are you?"

"I'm eighteen years old," I said. As I looked around at this business, I felt so at home and felt I could be part of this culture.

"Where are you working and what are you doing with your life?" she asked. I did not know what to say because I was not working a legitimate job. She continued, "They have a work program on Northern Boulevard next to Muhammad Temple. Why don't you go down and apply? When you come back to pick up your clothes, let me know how it went for you."

I went straight down to the work program, filled out all the forms, and was signed up for a training program. One week later I was in a class with eighteen other students. One of the students was white, but that was never an issue. They gave us classes on math, spelling, reading, writing, and hands-on mechanical skills building miniature airplanes. After three and a half weeks, we were tested in each area, including our hands-on skills. I tested low in reading, spelling, and writing. However, I placed at the top of my class in math, and first in hands-on mechanical skills. We were each given a certificate of completion. After I completed the training, I was given a job at Pan American Airlines, John F. Kennedy Airport, in Jamaica, Queens, cleaning the interior of airplanes.

This is a Picture of Pam American Graduating Class with certificate.

After starting this job, I stopped shooting heroin. Soon after I was told that I would be trained as an aircraft mechanic. I had taken all the tests and scored high and was promised a position as a trainee mechanic. I thought, *Wow, my dream of becoming an engineer might come true*! I was later told that cleaning the interior of the airplane was only the first step. However, I soon became frustrated with the system. During the work program, I was being passed over for many job opportunities.

Every day I came to work I watched the white boys working on Boeing 707s and Douglas DC-7s. One hangar could hold three aircraft. Pan American had shifts of mechanics working twenty-four hours a day. I worked rotating shifts and only saw two black mechanics. I began to surmise why there were not more black mechanics—this was discrimination at work.

Emotionally confused, I had no one to consult. I kept reflecting on my past and wanted to know where I was headed. As a little boy, I knew that engineers were builders and problem solvers. How would I be given this opportunity? Would my dream ever come true? I saw my current job as an avenue to become an aircraft mechanic, but I couldn't see how to transition from cleaning crew member to mechanical engineer. In my gut I also knew that prejudice was infecting the culture I was working in, living in, and there was no escape. I became frustrated, angry, and disappointed.

I decided I had to beat the white man at his own game, so I started selling drugs again. It didn't take long before I was picked up in Manhattan for possession. I knew better than to keep large amounts of drugs on me, so on that day I only had a small bag of marijuana. I was taken to the Manhattan House of Detention called The Tombs. After bailing myself out, I was soon picked up again, this time in Brooklyn, for the same thing. Eventually, the accumulation of my illegal activities caught up with me.

Down, but Not Out

Soon after, I was arrested at work for trafficking. The feds came to my boss with a warrant at Kennedy International Airport and took me to the Queens House of Detention. From there I was handcuffed and shackled and placed in a van full of inmates. As I looked out a window, I saw a long bridge to an island. Fear gripped my heart. *My God, what did I get myself into*? I was well aware of the notorious reputation of that most-hated prison—Ricker's Island. What was I to expect? What challenges would I face?

At that time, Ricker's was one of the world's most violent prisons. Just six miles from the Empire State Building, it is one of the largest, most complex, and expensive penal institutions in the world. Yet most New Yorkers cannot find it on a map. It housed about sixteen thousand inmates and eleven thousand correction officers. When I arrived in 1969, there was no correction, just punishment. I received no forms, nor was I offered classes on correction (if there were any opportunities for correction at that point, I was interested). Upon my arrival, I was immediately strip-searched and sprayed with some kind of disinfectant. In those days, you were allowed to wear the clothes on your back until sentencing.

Being in prison is grueling. It is hard to stay isolated and not belong to a group; belonging to a group afforded some protection. Fighting is the way of prison life. Someone was always trying to prey on me. I saw guys raped by other inmates and beaten, not just by inmates, but by prison guards as well. There were many gangs and groups, and all demanded I be a part of them—or else. There were the Latin Kings, the Skin Heads (an all white group), the Black Panthers, the Five Percenters, the Sunni Muslims, the Nation of Islam, the Gang Bangers, and the Christians. Of these groups, the Five Percenters caught my eye.

The Five Percenters began as an offshoot of the Nation of Islam back in 1964 and were led by Clarence 13X, who was a member of the Fruit of Islam in Mosque Number 7 under the tutelage of Malcolm X. The movement was founded when Clarence 13X was expelled from the mosque. It was claimed that he was expelled because he began to declare that he was Allah (God) in person. He rejected the notion that Wallace Fard was God Incarnate all by himself (another keystone of NOI theology). He began teaching that each black man was to be his own god.[3]

In some crazy, mixed-up, way, I could relate to what the Five Percenters were saying. I had low self-esteem, and their philosophies appealed to me. They said we didn't have to pray to any god because we are god or *little gods* who need to have the proper "knowledge of self." Five Percenters claim *esoteric* or secret knowledge that is loaded with conspiratorial propaganda. They also share the roots of black nationalism with the NOI. Some of the basic beliefs of the Five Percenters are:

1. Black people are the original race of people on earth.
2. Black people are the fathers and mothers of civilization.
3. Islam is a natural way of life, not a religion.
4. "Each one should teach one" according to his knowledge.
5. The black man is god and his proper name is ALLAH (Arm, Leg, Leg, Arm, Head).
6. The unified black family is the vital building block of the nation.[4]

Both the NOI and the Five Percenters hold to a racially-based ideology, which asserts that Christianity is a white man's religion fed to the blacks to deaden them from the effects of slavery. Both groups assert that the white race is a race of devils that cannot be redeemed, and civilization itself depends upon the success of the black races. Clarence 13X called himself Allah and was known by The Five Percenters as Father because he had founded the group. He didn't see a need to be a follower of Elijah Muhammad.

He simply took some of the lessons from NOI and adopted a new group name.

The name Five Percenters was derived from one of NOI's teachings, specifically lessons fifteen and sixteen. These taught that 85 percent of the population is made up of ignorant, unlearned, and uncivilized people, who need to be led (mostly churchgoers). This 85 percent is believed to have no "knowledge of self." Ten percent of the population has some knowledge of self (i.e., the real truth). However, they use this knowledge to wield control over the 85 percent instead of "liberating" them. For example, most Baptist preachers, such as Reverend Jesse Jackson, are believed to be in this category. Lastly, Clarence 13X considered the remaining 5 percent to be those who thought/believed like himself and his followers.

The "poor, righteous teachers" are the ones who possess knowledge of themselves, their origins, the way the world system really is, and the way in which the new world order will come about. Their job/mission is to educate the 85 percent to what this hidden or veiled knowledge really is (in the last few years, they have preferred to be called the Nation of Gods and Earths. The men are referred to as "gods" and the women are referred to as "earths").[5] This group is still around today in urban communities throughout America. There are other groups that are an offshoot of the Five Percenters, such as the Queen Nation of the Almighty Latin King.

While this group served to build me up emotionally, and to some degree spiritually, I also spent my time trying to get into some kind of program to help me obtain my General Educational Development certificate (GED). That never happened, but I tried to learn as much as I could on my own, reading anything educational I could find. It seemed that no attempt to better myself went unchallenged. One time I was in my cell reading and there was a call for head count, which meant that all inmates must stand in front of their cells while the prisons guards walked by and counted inmates. I was too engrossed in my book and didn't hear the call. The final count showed that one inmate was missing and the alarm went off. When I stepped out of my cell, I was shocked to see a black guard confronting me.

"Where were you when head count was called?"

"I was in my cell, reading and studying."

He replied, "Nigger, you will never learn anything." Then he and one other guard began to punch and beat me. I lost control and went into a rage. My boys (the other Five Percenters) jumped in to help. The alarm was sounded and the riot squad was called. They came with their riot gear on, consisting of helmets, face mask, and sticks. We had no weapons, not even the contraband that inmates typically hide. We were beaten, our cells were searched and stripped, then we were taken to solitary confinement called *the bent*. I was given thirty days in the bent, which meant being locked up twenty-four hours a day with no television or contact with any other inmate. I had no books to read and only a bed, a sink, and a toilet in my cell. Once a week we were let out for thirty minutes to take a shower.

To keep myself busy and to stay sane, I would do about one hundred jumping jacks, side-ups, and push-ups per day and shadow box to keep in shape. In prison life, you have to stay in fighting condition. I was completely lost spiritually and knew nothing about fighting in the spirit. I was confused and full of anger.

Start Again

Eventually, I began to see the Five Percenters as more of a gang that was not opposed to violence. The constant use of profanity grated against the morality that I had been exposed to as a child and still valued. For this reason, I left the Five Percenters and became involved in the Nation of Islam. It offered me the moral teaching, discipline, and direction that I felt I needed. Deep inside I knew that I had a special purpose in life. The NOI taught me how to live morally. They were disciplined men and didn't use profanity, nor were they stealing or fighting unless they were attacked first. Unfortunately, I did not see any Christian inmates setting the same example.

It was apparent that of all the groups of inmates, those who identified with the Nation of Islam were markedly more organized and well behaved. We followed all of the rules of the institution. I can remember one of the prison guards being comfortable enough to ask for my help. He had heard of a war being planned among several of the gangs. He knew that the members of the Nation of Islam were peaceful and would not partake of violence, except to protect ourselves. He asked me if I would be willing to negotiate some kind of peace between the groups. I went with other NOI members and talked to each group. We were able to come to a temporary agreement. Only the Latin Kings were reluctant to comply. They did not approve of the Nation of Islam cooperating peacefully with the rules of the institution.

Because I was heading the negotiations, the Latin Kings plotted to take me out (kill me). They were waiting to catch me alone. When the opportune time came, the group surrounded me. They were all speaking Spanish, so I had no way of knowing what they were saying. I knew the leader of the group and asked him, "What are they saying?"

"They want to take you out."

Fear gripped my heart. As my survival instinct took over, I opened my mouth and began to explain all the reasons why it did not make sense to kill me. I could hear the words coming out of my mouth, but I did not know where they were coming from.

"We are all in the same boat, locked up like animals," I said. "We can make this place run the way we want if we all work together. We all have the same enemy—the devil, the white man. He is using an old trick called *divide and conquer*. He wants us to kill ourselves. Listen, the members of the Nation of Islam are following the white man's rules and regulations to show him that we are civilized. The white man is really the one who is uncivilized."

I left unharmed.

Another trial by fire came whenever my oldest brother visited me. He was often high on drugs. He would offer to bring me drugs, but I would say, "Why do you think I am in here? Besides, I am surrounded by drugs in this place." I told him not visit me anymore if he wanted me to get high. About two weeks later, my twin sister came. She had a sickened look on her face. I knew something was seriously wrong. Our brother had been killed.

The prison officers informed me that I could not go to the funeral because it was out of state, but I was allowed to be taken in shackles and driven to the city morgue in downtown Manhattan. They took me to the morgue and pulled my brother's body out of a freezer. I looked at his face. It was hard and cold in my hands. I turned his head and saw he had been beaten, as if someone had hit him with a heavy object. Rage filled me as I realized he had been murdered. *Why my brother? Why not me?* At that moment, I knew I had to make a better life for myself. The only hope I had was in the teaching of the Honorable Elijah Muhammad. I realized that I would soon be released from prison, and I was determined to make my life count for something good.

A New Name

A few months after being released from Rikers, I moved back to Red Bank, New Jersey. Eventually I returned to the Nation of Islam. The first step in the process to become an official member of the NOI was to write to the Honorable Elijah Muhammad in Chicago at NOI headquarters and apply for my "X" (my new name). According to the NOI, my present last name was considered the last name of my ancestors' former slave masters. For example, if someone was named Johnson, he had come from the Johnson plantation. This is what we were taught by the Honorable Elijah Muhammad. If the application passed inspection, a certificate was drawn up and you were given the new family name, *X*. That X stands for *ex-slave*, or *unknown*. Our original family name was considered unknown because all blacks brought to America had been given American names. There was no way to trace our family history to our African tribe.

Then there were the lessons. After receiving a new name, the first lesson assigned was a recitation called, The Student Enrollment. Initiates are required to learn it verbatim and recite it from memory to an elder. Once the question and answer is recited one hundred percent accurately, initiates write to headquarters in Chicago and wait for lesson number 2.

MUHAMMAD'S MOSQUE NO. 2
5335 South Greenwood Avenue
Chicago, Illinois 60615
July 18, 1972

Mr. Alexis X Johnson
Red Bank, New Jersey

As-Salaam-Alaikum:

In the Name of Almighty Allah, The Beneficent, The Most Merciful Saviour; Sole Master of the Day of Judgment. We forever thank Allah for His Last Messenger, our beloved Leader and Teacher: THE HONORABLE ELIJAH MUHAMMAD.

Dear Brother/Sister:

Your Form has passed the Laborers' Inspection. We hope it will be approved by Allah.

Enclosed are ten Student Enrollment Questions. Please answer these questions and send us a copy of your answers.

If you need any help in answering these questions, please see your Mosque Secretary for assistance.

Be sure that your full name, address, city, state and the date appears on your paper.

You will also find enclosed a list of Actual Facts. These are for you to learn by heart; you need not send us a copy of them.

May the peace and blessings from Allah be upon you.

As-Salaam-Alaikum:
Your Sister,
Margary Hassain
Margary Hassain
Secretary

mh/m
encl.

July 18, 1972/ letter

July 18, 1972, I officially became a member of the NOI and was known as Alexis X, a registered member of Muhammad Temple Number 25 in Newark, New Jersey. The following year I was married. My wife was an excellent Muslim woman and Muslim wife. She supported my involvement in the NOI, which had excellent family values programs. There were programs set up in every temple for men and women. Women attended MGT classes (Muslim Girls Training). They were taught that they are the mothers of civilization and instructed on how to conduct themselves accordingly.

Another program called the GCC (General Civilization Classes) taught women how to cook, sew, take care of their children, and treat their husbands. There were taught that a Muslim woman should talk and walk with dignity and respect. The Honorable Elijah Muhammad taught that no nation can rise any higher than its women. The women were taught that they, in turn, could rise as high as their talents would allow them. However, a woman's talents and interests were to stay within the framework of the NOI.

The men's program, in which I was involved as a student, was called the Fruit of Islam (FOI). We were taught that men are the protectors and maintainers of their families. All men were required to attend training classes, including the martial arts. Because we were taught by the Honorable Elijah Muhammad to obey the laws of the government, members of the FOI were not allowed to carry a weapon but were taught to use self-defense if necessary. It was also a way of empowerment, to build self-esteem.

The FOI classes also taught entrepreneurship, another avenue of empowerment. The Honorable Elijah Muhammad stood solely for the empowerment of the black man. He would say, "Up, you mighty nation; you can accomplish what you will." He taught us to "do for self," and not depend on the white man. Because of this teaching many doors opened for me.

Achieving full-time employment was monumental for my self-esteem. I was selling products for the Nation of Islam, including the newspaper Mr. Muhammad Speaks, bean pies, hundreds of pounds of fish, and cookies. I worked in my own corner of a grocery/fish market. The concepts of personal responsibility and providing for yourself were always reinforced in the temple.

Through the NOI, I learned the correlation between caring for self and caring for others. I had to have my own house in order before I could be of service to my brother. Somehow this aspect of "loving others as yourself" seemed to be lost in the Christian church, as I remember it. Christians are supposed to put others first and deny self. The trouble I had was I didn't know who "myself" was supposed to be. I didn't know who I was meant to be, nor was I given opportunities or direction to really find out. But through the opportunities and tutelage of the NOI, I had accomplished much. I started my own business, bought a pickup truck, and was doing all kinds of odd jobs. Eventually, I started my own painting business (it lasted for over thirty years and employed many people).

The unfortunate thing about being empowered was the underlying message: I had to do it "to beat the white man." This enabled me to justify my resentments. Furthermore, when it came to the white man, there was no teaching regarding forgiveness. In fact the NOI taught, and continues to teach, that white people are actually devils who cannot be redeemed. We were taught that white men were created to promulgate injustices solely for the benefit of the black race (the only human race with a soul), so that the black race could earn its freedom, i.e., its salvation. That is the actual worldview held by the NOI. This racially-based theology colored everything we worked toward. It provided solidarity as we continued to suffer racial victimization. It was a vicious circle of logic that made sense of the world as I knew it.

Moving Up

I had started attending Muhammad's Temple (Muhammad's Mosque) in Asbury Park on a regular basis. It was a sub-branch of Muhammad's Temple Number 25, Newark, New Jersey. The head minister of temple Number 25 was Minister James Shabass. Sadly, he was killed in an internal power struggle within the organization. I remember the meetings that were called in the wake of his death.

Elijah Muhammad addressed the issue by reminding us that the white man, the devil, was doing his job by sowing divisions among us and by having us fight and kill each other. In spite of this controversy, my faith in the organization wasn't shaken. It was easy to turn a blind eye or blame such trouble on others when I was finding acceptance and reaping the rewards of learning personal responsibility for the first time in my life. My family saw a big change in me for the better. As far as I was concerned, all was well with my soul and I was on the path to heaven.

The NOI was filling the void in my life that had not been met by the Christian church. They also provided a deep sense of spirituality. The power struggle, however, was very confusing. Because the preaching for the empowerment of black people specifically—as opposed to all people—was so racially charged, we had to submit to a body search before attending services at the mosque. The minister faced the danger of being challenged by members of the community at any moment. Men and women were directed into two different rooms; their pockets were searched, then they were patted down for weapons.

Upon gaining admittance to the mosque, the men are seated on one side of the room and the women on the other. The men of FOI are seated in the front of the men's section, facing the audience, to serve as security.

On the front platform was a large blackboard with a picture of the cross on the left, which stood for Christianity. On the right was a picture of the star and crescent, which stood for Islam, and the words "Freedom, Justice, and Equality." In the middle of the blackboard was written, "Which one would you choose: Islam or Christianity?" The NOI was clearly making race a more predominant issue than one's religion, while indicting the Christian church for the injustices suffered by blacks.

The responsibility does not fall entirely upon the Christian church, but at that time there was a very powerful cultural divide within America that the Christian churches were not positioned to address. Instead of standing against the culture, the church was a reflection of the culture. If you were a black man, where would you have felt more understood?

The Christian church simply did not provide a safe haven for blacks to recover from the injustices thrust upon them. Thus, racism birthed the Nation of Islam in America. Blacks began to run to black nationalism movements as a means to survive in a hostile culture that was fraught with fear. Many blacks no longer identified with the church nor saw it as a place of hope for their issues. The Nation of Islam began to fill the void of relevance for many. For me, these cultural influences were some of the very reasons I had become involved in the Nation of Islam.

We were trained to recruit others into NOI by witnessing on the street and going door-to-door, sharing the message of the Honorable Elijah Muhammad, just as I had seen done on the streets of Red Bank. I was always amazed how many

Christians were not able to defend their faith. I remember volunteering to serve at a youth correctional facility called Jamesbury Home for Boys located in Jamesbury, New Jersey. I informed the pastor that I had only come to help, but of course I had my own agenda. They had been meeting on a weekly basis for Bible study, and I was invited to address the boys, even though the minister knew I was a member of the NOI. That was a gracious gesture on his part, but it had repercussions for which he was unprepared. Eventually, I began to challenge his ideas about the Bible in front of the youth. His faith was so weak that he began to question his own belief. Eventually, I took over the whole class and began teaching regularly about the NOI.

In 1973 I became a minister in the Nation of Islam and an assistant minister in the local mosque in Asbury Park. I was assistant minister there for two and a half years. I made frequent trips to Muhammad's Mosque #7 in New York City to sit under the teaching of Minister Louis Farrakhan, who was the national representative of Elijah Muhammad. At that time there was a controversy about the meaning of his name. Once while sitting in class I asked him, "Brother Minister (as we referred to him), what does your name mean and did the Honorable Elijah Muhammad give you that name?"

"Brother, yes, the Honorable Elijah Muhammad gave me my name, but he did not tell me what that name meant."

I could not have guessed the tremendous impact this mysterious man would have twenty years later upon the African American community and African American churches.

I had the opportunity to travel to Chicago a few times to attend the Nation of Islam's annual Savior's Day Convention held at the old Armory on South Giles Avenue, then the South Central Gymnasium. Savior's Day is a most important day and considered a holy day of obligatory observance by the NOI. It was a day to celebrate the coming of our (NOI) savior, Master W. D. Fard Muhammad, who first conceived the NOI, originally called the Lost Found Nation of Islam, in 1930.

Once a year the members of the NOI would have a chance to hear and see, in person, the Honorable Elijah Muhammad. He was Master Fard Muhammad's successor. I was present at what would be the last Savior's Day sermon ever given by Elijah Muhammad on February 26, 1974. Though he was physically ill and weakened with age, he spoke powerfully about the reality of God and the coming of a savior—a man we could see face-to-face and not a spook or some spirit. He stated that every time we looked at a black man, we were looking at God. By this time, I was now completely submerged in my new identity and proud of the opportunities and experiences I had found within the Islamic community. It was easy for the charisma of Elijah Muhammad to confirm the deep and hidden wisdom concerning the coming victory of the black race over "Yakub's trouble," or the evil within the white race.

By 1974, I started reading the Qur'an, the Muslim holy book, and other Islamic books. They did not coincide with some of Mr. Muhammad's teachings, but they were permitted reading. It was around this time that Elijah Muhammad's son, Wallace D. Muhammad, became supreme minister of the Nation of Islam. Immediately he was given authority to teach all the ministers of the NOI, probably to prepare the members for his transition after the death of his father.

I was in Chicago on February 26, 1975, at the Savior Day Convention the day after Elijah Muhammad died. He was previously hospitalized for asthma and had been admitted with a heart-related condition. Wallace D. Muhammad was scheduled to speak in his place. I was in a special meeting for ministers the morning before the convention when he informed all the ministers and leaders that his father was physically dead. On that day, Wallace D. Muhammad was introduced as the leader of the Nation of Islam. The convention proceeded as usual. Soon after Supreme Minister Wallace D. Muhammad began to reinterpret the teaching and lessons of his father, he admitted to mistakes his father had made, stating that his father was wrong for teaching that white people are devils. In addition, he began to teach the NOI community that the story of Yakub was a myth.

Wallace D. Muhammad began to use his youth and charisma to transition the members of the NOI in a new direction—into mainstream Islam (aka the Sunni sect). In 1976, he changed the name of the Nation of Islam to the World Community of Al-Islam in the West, and his title became that of Chief imam. His goal was to bring the African American Muslims in touch with the essentials of mainstream Muslim life and identity. He wanted us to be more in line with the tenets required by the authentic sources of the religion of Islam, the Holy Qur'an and the life example of the Prophet Muhammad. After formally embracing the orthodox Sunni sect, he changed his name to Warith Deen Muhammad, as he is now known.

I, too, embraced the teaching of imam Warith Deen Muhammad, and that same year I became a Sunni Muslim, as did many other NOI members. I had my name legally changed to Khalif Majid Hasan.

I continued in my Islamic studies of mainstream Islam, including reading the Holy Qur'an. Since no Muslim can pray properly in English, I began to learn my prayers in Arabic. I sat in classes under imams from Egypt and Saudi Arabia, who would teach the recitation of the Holy Qur'an for the purpose of prayer. I also read and studied as many *hadiths* as I could (hadiths are oral traditions relating to the words and deeds of the Prophet Muhammad).

Because of my previous studies, I quickly obtained the status of imam (community leader or mosque leader) and began to preach sermons in the mosque at Asbury Park and to lead in congregational prayers. I took advantage of opportunities to present the teachings of Islam on college campuses, such as Brookdale Community College in Lincroft, New Jersey, and Rutgers University in New Brunswick, as well as in community groups such as the local chapter of the NAACP, which met in Red Bank. Sometimes we met in homes, other times in a rented church hall. Moreover, I began preaching very strongly against Christianity.

A Spiritual Challenge

Around 1985, I began discussing Islam with my family, particularly my sisters, who were devoted and well-informed Christians. We would discuss the doctrine of the Trinity. How could he be one and three at the same time? I read the Bible from Genesis to Revelation, but I could not comprehend the concept of three-in-one. Islam teaches that God (Allah) is one, and that there is no God except for him. How could Jesus, who was a man, be God? How can God be constrained to flesh and blood? How could Jesus be the Son of God? This did not make any sense to me.

My twin sister, Amelia, was attending a Christian college called Christ for the Nations in Texas. We talked over the phone and wrote letters to each other frequently. She wrote about her views on Jesus Christ as the Son of God, and I wrote about Jesus as a prophet of God from an Islamic perspective.

I remember her sharing the idea that Jesus died on the cross for my sins. I told her that Muslims do not believe one man can die for the sins of the world, just as Muslims do not believe that one man's sin can cause all men to be sinners. Muslims believe that it was *someone else* who was on the cross, not the prophet Jesus. Rather than take the crucifixion of Jesus as historical fact, they deduce that the substitution was necessary in order to uphold a higher spiritual principle, rather than blood atonement.

One day my sister and I were on the phone talking about this very thing when I said to her, "If Jesus did die on the cross, then the only thing he did was commit suicide." That was as far as my understanding could take me. She didn't try to convince me, but she was confident and told me so.

"Regardless of what you say or believe, Jesus died for your sins and he loves you. And someday you are going to accept Jesus Christ as your savior and become a Christian."

"Not in a million years!" I said. We continued to write and call each other.

In 1986, Amelia called. "I have been praying for you and I am asking you to pray and ask God if he won't show you that Jesus Christ *is* the Son of God, and how he could possibly have died on the cross for your sins." I accepted her challenge because I loved challenges and I was confident in Islam!

Allah said in the Qur'an in Surah CXII, (chapter 112 of *Ikhlas* or Purity of Faith), "In the name of God, Most Gracious, Most Merciful, say: He is God, the One and Only; God, the Eternal, Absolute; He begetteth not, nor is He begotten; And there none like unto Him" (translation by A. Yusuf Ali). I recited this prayer every day. I had confidence and submitted myself to God to show me if Christ had died for my sins, and if so then I would become a Christian. If not, I would teach and promote Islam like never before! I was safely submitted to God, and whatever the outcome, I was confident that God would have his way.

I began praying that prayer regularly. Unbeknown to me, hundreds of people were praying for my conversion. One evening, I was standing in front of a 7-Eleven convenience store in the Pine Brook section of Eatontown, New Jersey. A man approached me and asked for directions to a particular church. I asked him if he knew anyone there. He proceeded to name my oldest sister and some of her children. By my reaction he realized who I was and said, "Oh, you are that Muslim we've been praying for. I call you out of that religion!"

"You do not have to pray for me; Islam is my religion, and Allah is my God," I insisted. As I looked back at this man, a strange feeling came over me. (That man was none other than Bishop Dr. Donald Hilliard Jr. of Cathedral International, Perth Amboy, New Jersey).

I kept challenging God with my prayers, and strange things began to happen. One Sunday, I was in the mosque giving a *khutbah* (sermon) on the story of Christmas and the Christian belief about the birth of Christ. I quoted scriptures from the Bible and what Christians have to say about the birth of Jesus.

> And in the sixth month the angel Gabriel was sent from God unto a city of Galilee, named Nazareth, to a virgin espoused to a man whose name was Joseph, of the house of David; and the virgin's name was Mary. And the angel came in unto her, and said, "Hail thou that art highly favored, the Lord is with thee: blessed art thou among women." And when she saw him, she was troubled at his saying, and cast in her mind what manner of salutation this should be. And the angel said unto her, "Fear not, Mary: for thou hast found favor with God." And, behold thou shall conceive in thy womb, and bring forth a son, and shalt call his name JESUS." He shall be great, and

> shall be called the Son of the Highest: and Lord God shall give unto him the throne of his father David.
>
> —Luke 1:26-35 KJV

After I finished reading, something strange began to happen inside of me. There I was a Muslim leader standing in an Islamic mosque quoting from the Gospel of Saint Luke in the hearing of Muslim men and women that Jesus is the Son of the Highest (God). I knew I didn't believe what I was reading, but as I heard the words in my own ears they seemed to be spoken by a higher authority. I could not explain it intellectually, but my heart began to race.

I continued to talk about the birth of Jesus from an Islamic perspective.

> Behold! The angels said, "O Mary! God giveth thee Glad tidings of a Word from Him: his name Will be Christ Jesus, The son of Mary, held in honour In this world and the Hereafter And of (the company of) those Nearest to God; He shall speak to the people In childhood and in maturity. And he shall be (of the company) Of the righteous." She said; "O my Lord! How shall I have a son When no man hath touched me?" He said; "Even so: God createth What He willeth: When He hath decreed A Plan, He but saith To it, 'Be,' and it is! Surah 3:45-47, from the chapter called Al-i-Imran (The Family of Imran), in the Qur'an. (A. Yusuf Ali translation)

I said that Islam has no problems with the virgin birth. Islam teaches that God (Allah) first created man out of nothing (clay), then he made woman out of man. He has completed the process by making a man (baby) without a man. Because Jesus was made with God's creative word "Be," he was called a "Word from God." However, Islam rejects the concept of Jesus as the Son of God.

I had recited and explained these verses many times and had heard imams and Islamic scholars explain them. Yet as I spoke, deep within my heart doubt arose for the first time. I felt a contradiction, but I could not identify it. I intensified my study of the Bible, comparing references to Jesus in the Bible with the ones in the Qur'an.

My recitation of the Qur'an in Arabic was not articulate or fluent. However, it was understandable and acceptable enough to lead prayer in a mosque. I remember leading *Jumah* prayer (Friday congregational prayer) at the mosque in Asbury Park. I recited the first *surah* (character) of the Qur'an called *Al-Fatiha* (the Opening), which is the most often repeated prayer. I had delivered this surah by memory many times before. However, strangely, I could not remember every word. The recitation of the Qur'an is supposed to be word for word; no word can be changed or omitted.

While I was praying I could hear a Muslim brother behind me trying to correct me, but I was in a daze. I could not remember the prayers that I had recited for years. Afterwards, this brother approached me. He was an Egyptian Muslim who was fluent in Arabic and in the recitation of the Qur'an and had visited the Jumah prayer many times before. I have never forgotten his words. He said, "Brother, Allah is not going to hear our prayers." He was reminding me of my responsibility as imam.

The imam is the one who stands in front, and whom everyone else follows as he leads prayer. Very much like a priest, the responsibility for the entire prayer is upon him. If he is incorrect, the prayers of those praying with him are invalid, rejected. His words rang in my ears. And the weight of the responsibility was too great for me to bear. That day I made a decision that I would never lead prayer in the mosque again. Something was happening to me, but I did not know what. As much as I loved Islam, doubts began to enter my mind. My life as a Muslim began to quickly unravel.

A New Relationship

One day I received a letter from my twin sister inviting me to attend her graduation ceremony for her Associate Arts degree in Practical Theology from Christ for the Nations Institute. I telephoned my sister and said, "I believe this trip could be a turning point in my life. I have been praying that prayer you asked me to pray. When I come back I will either be a Christian, or I will rededicate my life to Islam."

The day came and my sister met me at the airport and took me to the school of Christ for the Nations. We entered the auditorium to overflowing songs and praise as the people worshipped God. It felt very different to me. I had never been in a service with such meaning, and I could sense something authentic and special.

After the service, my sister introduced me to her friend, Joseph, who was a former Muslim from Africa. As we became better acquainted, he began to explain why he had become a Christian. He had been raised a Muslim in a tribe that mixed old tribal practices with Islamic theology (Folk Islam). He shared an awesome testimony: he was the first in his family who came to know Jesus Christ as his personal savior.*

The next day, my sister introduced me to an Egyptian student who was a former Muslim. I will never forget him. I was impressed because he came from a long line of Muslims. He knew Islam, the Qur'an, and was fluent in Arabic as well as Quranic Arabic. He shared with me Philippians 2:5-8, "Let this mind be in you, which was also in Christ Jesus: Who being in the form of God thought it not robbery to be equal with God...." He told me that God loved us so much, he came himself in the very person of Jesus Christ to die on the cross for our sins, leaving his high throne and giving up his authority to take on human form and become a servant.

He painted a picture for me of a personal and intimate God. He said his mother had told him, "If you denounce Christianity, I will give you one million dollars." (For a Muslim to confess that Jesus is the Son of God is considered *shirk,* idolatry in Islam). She said, "Son, since you do not denounce Christianity, then from this day forward you are no longer my son: I consider you dead." He told his mother he would never deny Jesus Christ as the Son of God, because Jesus was his Savior. He told me how he wept and suffered as his whole family turned their backs on him. His words touched my heart deeply.⁺

The next day, my sister took me to her church. It was very small. As I entered, I sat at the back of the room. Everyone was singing, praising, and worshipping God. Suddenly, a man sitting in the last row behind me began to speak in a strange way. As he continued I could feel something and I sensed that he was somehow talking to me, but I could not understand his words. Then I heard a voice within me say, "I am the God that you have been looking for; I am the God of Abraham, Isaac, and Jacob. I am your God."

I sat there, convinced within myself to accept the authority of Jesus Christ and embrace Him as my Savior. Even today, I do not remember anything the speaker (pastor) said. I only remember the end of his message, and somehow I found myself at the front of the church. Standing there, the pastor asked me, "Why are you here? What do you want from God?"

"I do not understand this concept of the Trinity, God being three in one, I just do not understand," I replied.

"Understanding will come later. You must first acknowledge your faith in Jesus Christ."

That very day I renounced Islam. Moreover, I realized I was a sinner and needed a Savior. The pastor shared scripture with me.

> That if you confess with your mouth the Lord Jesus and believe in your heart that God raised Him from the dead, you will be saved.
>
> —Romans 10:9 NKJV

Then he led me in a prayer of acceptance—acceptance of the free gift of salvation given to us through the authority of Jesus Christ. Anyone can pray to receive salvation. My prayer was something like this:

> Father, in the name of Jesus Christ, I come unto You just as I am. I am a sinner. I have sinned against You and against heaven. I ask you, Lord Jesus, to forgive me and to come into my heart and save my soul. Let me be born again by the Spirit of the living God. I give my life to you, Lord Jesus. I do believe that you are the Son of God. I give you thanks and praise and honor for redeeming me by your precious blood.

After praying that prayer, I felt a ton of weight lifting off of me. I was a changed man inside. I knew I no longer had to try to live by some religious law or try to be good enough to please God or to get to heaven. I was no longer weighing the difference between human souls in my heart and mind. I was no longer conflicted about who was worthy of salvation. I could finally see the big picture of God's salvation plan for *all* mankind, not according to race or creed. I could appreciate its simplicity. The gospel of Jesus Christ, which supersedes all religions, had finally reached me.

> For God so loved the world that He gave His only begotten Son, that whoever believes in Him should not perish but have everlasting life.
>
> —John 3:16 NKJV

Our relationship with God is not based upon having secret knowledge or adhering to a set of laws, but by acknowledging and receiving the gift of the relationship.

> If you confess with your mouth the Lord Jesus and believe in your heart that God has raised Him from the dead, you will be saved. For with the heart one believes unto righteousness, and with the mouth confession is made unto salvation.
>
> —Romans 10:9-10, 13 NKJV

Hallelujah! To God be all praise and honor!

I came back to New Jersey a changed man. My children thought I was crazy. I had taught them and raised them as Muslims; to them I seemed to be a confused man. However, I began to daily share with them my new life in Christ Jesus. I was full of joy and could not hold back my newfound faith.

My former Muslim brothers saw a change in me. Many of them were not happy about my conversion. Some wanted me dead. My best friend simply couldn't believe it and invited me to the mosque to pray. We went to the mosque one Friday for *Jumah*, the most important day and prayer of the week. When it was time for the congregation to rise for prayer, I remained seated. My Muslim friend was astonished that I had remained seated. He looked at me and said, "What are you doing? Stand up and worship and pray to Allah."

I said to him kindly, "I cannot. I am now a Christian."

The Muslim brothers were angry with me and said, "You came in here and disrespected our mosque. Do not come back. You are not welcome."

My life now belonged to Jesus. Soon, I became involved with a ministry called Good News for the Crescent World. I began to travel throughout the state of New Jersey and different parts of the country sharing my testimony. I have spoken in many churches where the congregation was predominately white. As of this writing, I am the assistant pastor of Tabernacle of Glory Church in Asbury Park.

The most remarkable part of my journey is that I have been a volunteer at the Monmouth County Correctional Institute in Freehold, New Jersey, for the past thirteen years, conducting Bible studies. That facility is a bit different from the way I remember it as a teenager! Today there are inmates from different parts of the world. Each week I work with inmates from many different nationalities and backgrounds. Truly, the foreign mission field has come to America! I have seen Muslims come to the saving knowledge of Jesus Christ in prison. God is good! What the devil meant for evil—in my life and in the lives these inmates—God has turned around for good. Forty-three years ago I was an inmate there, locked up in the old section of the correctional institute. Now, praise be to God, I have returned with the good news of Christ. Hallelujah!

CHAPTER TWO

History of a Counterfeit Nation

HERE IS AN outline of the history of the Nation of Islam as taught to me by Elijah Muhammad.[6]

A The Nation of Islam (NOI)
1. Originally called the Lost Found Nation of Islam.
2. Founded July 4, 1930, in the poorest community in Detroit, Michigan, called Black Bottom.

B Fard Muhammad
1. Founder.
2. He came as a peddler of clothing and silk. He was known as:
   - i. W. D. Fard
   - ii. Wallace D. Fard
   - iii. W. Fard Muhammad
   - iv. Fard Muhammad
   - v. Wali Fard or Mr. Fard

vi. He was later known by his earlier converts as Master Fard Muhammad
vii. Allah (God) in person

3. Fard Muhammad was born in Mecca, Arabia, on February 26, 1877.
4. He said that his father was a wise black scientist who prepared him for this mission.
5. His mother was an Armenian blonde-haired woman whom he referred to as the devil.†
6. He was well versed in the Bible, Qur'an, history, mathematics, and astronomy. He spoke sixteen languages and wrote ten perfectly.
7. He started having meetings in homes and opened up a temple called Temple No. 1 in Detroit, Michigan.

C Elijah Muhammad

1. Formerly known as Elijah Poole, born October 7, 1897, in Sandersville, Georgia, the son a Baptist preacher.

    i. His mother's name was Maria, which is the Spanish version of Mary.
    ii. He was the 7th of thirteen children.
    iii. His paternal grandfather called him Elijah the Prophet when he was a little boy.
    iv. He only had a third grade education.
    v. He married at the age of twenty-five and had children.

2. The first surname given to Elijah by his teacher Fard Muhammad was Karriem (noble).
3. Elijah was Fard Muhammad's best student. Fard Muhammad later changed Elijah Karriem's name to Elijah Muhammad when he was chosen to be the

Supreme Minister of the Nation of Islam in 1930. Muhammad means praiseworthy.

4. In 1934, after leading the NOI for three years and four months, Fard Muhammad disappeared. It is still disputed where Fard Muhammad went. It is alleged by the NOI that he left because he said his job was done.
    i. He left the Nation of Islam in the hands of Elijah Muhammad.
    ii. He left many of his lessons and teachings with Elijah Muhammad along with the Qur'an written in Arabic.

D Elijah Muhammad's Mission

1. After Fard Muhammad's departure:
    i. Elijah began to tell his followers and the world that Fard Muhammad was not merely a prophet.
    ii. He began to teach that Fard Muhammad was God in person, the long awaited Mahdi of the Muslim world and the Messiah of the Christians.
    iii. He declared to all that he (Elijah) was the Messenger of Allah (God).
    iv. He began to teach that he was the Elijah of Malachi chapter 3:1;4:5-6.
    v. He taught about the resurrection of the dead, not in physical resurrection but in mental resurrection.
    vi. He called his people so-called Negroes.
    vii. His mission was to establish a separate state or territory for his own people.
    viii. He began to publish a weekly newspaper out of Detroit, Michigan, called *The Final Call to Islam* (1934).

1. It provided lessons and information regarding the coming of a Messiah.
2. He hosted many question and answer sessions with Bible and Qur'an scriptures to back up his statements.

E Nation of Islam Headquarters

1. Due to disputes and arrests concerning his fight for equal educational rights for Muslims, Elijah Muhammad moved to Chicago, Illinois, in September of 1934.
2. There he established the national headquarters of NOI, called Temple No. 2.

F The Building of a Nation

1. Economic development.
2. 35,000 acres of farmland purchased in Georgia, Michigan, and Alabama.

   i. Produced beef, lamb, produce, chickens, eggs, and dairy products.
   ii. Slaughtering and packaging stores.
   iii. Wholesale business.
   iv. Food processing cannery.
   v. A fleet of NOI tractor trailer trucks.
   vi. Various retail outlets.
   vii. Bakeries, supermarkets, restaurants, bookstores, and more.

G The Building of Homes

1. Privately owned homes by NOI.
2. Apartment buildings.

H Clothing Factory

1. Produced by their own farms by raising cotton, wool, and hides.
2. Clothing stores.

I He united with other black leaders and established a black bank called Guarantee Bank.

J Printing Press

1. A weekly newspaper called *Mr. Muhammad Speaks* was launched in 1961. Circulation grew to one million copies a week by 1972.
   - i. This publication provided full-time jobs in the thousands.
     - a. Editor-in-Chief.
     - b. Managing Editor.
     - c. Many other managers.
     - d. Staff writers.
     - e. Graphic designers.
     - f. Drivers.
     - g. Newspaper salesmen.
     - h. Tractor trailer drivers.
     - i. Office workers.
     - j. Warehouse workers.

K International Trade

1. Import and export business with Middle Eastern and Asian countries and all over Africa.
   - i. Imported shiploads of fish, enabling many Muslims to open up their own markets.

L By 1972, the Nation of Islam as an incorporated enterprise was estimated to own businesses worth approximately eighty million dollars, all under the direct leadership of Elijah Muhammad.

M Muhammad University of Islam (MUI)

1. Private schools were set up throughout the United States.
2. By 1975 there were forty-four Muhammad universities throughout the country.
3. Grades pre-K – 12th grade.
4. Subjects taught ranged from a basic education to Arabic, astronomy, mathematics, science, and engineering.
5. All classes were geared towards college preparation.
6. The history of the NOI and its beliefs were taught.
7. Dress code for MUI.

    i. Girls' heads had to be covered and long dresses were to be worn.
    ii. Boys wore white shirts and bow ties, with black or blue pants.

N Military Unit of the Nation of Islam (NOI)

1. Fruit of Islam (FOI)

    i. One Supreme Captain over the NOI.
    ii. Regional captains.
    iii. Local captains.
    iv. Lieutenants.
    v. Foot soldiers.

2. Responsibilities of the FOI

    i. To protect and fulfill the plans, goals, and objectives of the NOI.
    ii. No member of the FOI is allowed to carry a weapon.

   iii. FOI are taught not to attack anyone. However, if attacked, defend yourselves.
   iv. FOI are taught how to defend themselves if attacked.
   v. FOI are taught marching and precision drilling.
   vi. FOI are taught how to be husbands and fathers and how to respect women.
   vii. All FOI must respect the law and must be employed or self-employed.
   viii. All FOI must be in good standing by practicing the restrictive laws of Islam as taught by Elijah Muhammad.

O Muslim Girls' Training (MGT) and General Civilization Classes (GCC)

1. National MGT Captain.
2. Regional Captain.
3. Local Captain.
4. Lieutenants.
5. Foot soldiers.
6. Responsibilities of MGT and GCC
   i. MGT–the young girls are taught that they are the mothers of civilization and that a people or nation can rise no higher than its women.
   ii. GCC–the women are taught how to respect and take care of their husbands, cook, keep house, and raise their children.

7. MGT and GCC Rights
   i. She can rise as high as her talents will allow.
   ii. Her talents and interests must stay within the framework of the NOI.

P Malcolm X

1. Formerly known as Malcolm Little.
    - i. Born May 19, 1925, in Omaha, Nebraska.
    - ii. Son of Reverend Earl Little, a Baptist preacher.
    - iii. In 1952, Malcolm X started attending Temple No. 1 in Detroit.
    - iv. In 1953, Malcolm X became Assistant Minister of Temple No. 1.
    - v. Malcolm X traveled all over the country helping Elijah Muhammad establish NOI temples.
    - vi. In June of 1954, Elijah Muhammad appointed Malcolm X as the Minister of Temple No. 7 in New York City.
    - vii. Later Malcolm X was appointed National Representative of the NOI.

2. Malcolm X suspended from NOI.
    - i. Suspension in 1964.
    - ii. March 8, 1964, Malcolm announced his formal break from the NOI.
    - iii. In 1964 Malcolm X made pilgrimage to Mecca.
    - iv. In 1964 Malcolm X changed name to El-Hajj Malik El- Shabazz.
    - v. In 1965 El-Hajj Malik El-Shabazz established Muslim Mosque Inc. in New York City.
    - vi. In 1965 Malcolm was assassinated.

Q Minister Louis Farrakhan

1. Born Louis Eugene Wolcot.
2. Birth date May 11, 1933.
    - i. Place: Bronx, New York.

3. His mother was born in the Caribbean, and his father was from Jamaica.
4. He was raised a member of the Protestant Episcopal Church.
5. Education
    i. High School: Roxbury section of Boston.
        a. Started playing the violin at age five.
        b. Attended Winston Salem Teacher's College in North Carolina.
6. Married in 1953
    i. Started supporting his family in show business.
    ii. He and his wife joined the NOI in 1955.
7. Served briefly under Malcolm X in New York.
8. Held the office of Lieutenant and Captain of the FOI.
9. Given the name Farrakhan by Elijah Muhammad.
10. In 1967, he was appointed National Representative of Elijah Muhammad.

I learned the theology of the NOI bit by bit as I continued attending the meetings at the mosque. The ministers there would never preach, but rather, teach. Occasionally the teaching was taken from the Bible and Qur'an. We were taught how to interpret key passages, such as when God spoke to Abram and said,

> Know for a surety that thy seed shall be a stranger in a land that is not theirs, and shall serve them; and they shall afflict them four hundred years. And also that nation whom they shall serve, will I judge: and afterward they shall come out with great substance.
>
> —Genesis 15:13 KJV

We were taught that the people God was talking about were the so-called American Negroes, and that white men were our slave masters, and that America is the "strange land" we were brought to when we were taken out of our own land. Therefore, God's intention was to punish our slave masters.

We were taught that God came himself in July 1930 in the person of Master W. Fard Muhammad, Allah (God) in person. He was the "Son of Man," the "Christ," the "Comforter" that the prophets of old had prophesied about. One of the Scripture references that Fard used to teach about his coming was,

> For as the lightning cometh out of the east, and shineth even unto the west, so shall also the coming of the Son of Man be.
>
> —Matthew 24:27 KJV

We were taught that when the Son of Man came to Earth, (meaning, W. D. Fard Muhammad), he would sit to judge the devil, the white man. The Son of Man is not a spirit, we were taught, but flesh and blood. Where would this Son be coming from? We were taught that the Prophet Jesus had said about him; "He will come from the east," (Matthew 24:27). Islam came from the East, as did all of the former prophets mentioned in the Scriptures. We were taught in the Mosque that Jesus had foretold the coming of Islam. But there were many other distorted teachings...

We were taught the history of the black nation and that the blacks are the original people of the earth. They were god-men, the makers of everything: sun, moon, stars—and the makers of the white race. We were taught that the black man (the race) impacts history once every 25,000 years. It is done by twenty-four black scientists who sit on the throne: "Around the throne were twenty-four thrones, and on the thrones I saw twenty-four elders sitting" (Revelation 4:4 NKJV). One acts as judge or God (Allah) for the other twenty-three, who actually direct the work of raising up the black nation on earth. The teaching of the twenty-four elders is put into a book; when the time comes on earth for that new truth to be revealed, the book is introduced into our history, as were the Bible and Qur'an. According to this teaching, there is significance to the number twenty-four, the scientists, and the reference to 25,000 years. The number twenty-four is used in accordance with the hours of a day; the 25,000 is the measurement of the circumference of our planet around the equator (longitude) and across the poles of the Arctic and Antarctic circles (latitude). The change made in the rotation of the planet at the poles is about one minute a year and takes 25,000 years to bring about a complete change in the region of the poles. The actual poles are inclined 23 1/2 degrees (nearly twenty-four) to the planet of its orbit. (The planet is not exactly 25,000 miles in circumference; the correct measurement is 24,896 miles and we, according to astronomy, do not have a full 24-hour day, but 23 hours, 56 minutes and 46 seconds. But the emphasis on numbers adds to the intrigue and seems like wisdom to the unlearned). And this is what we were taught with authority by Elijah Muhammad himself.

Elijah Muhammad declared to us that Allah (meaning, Master Fard Muhammad) had taught him that our history goes back to sixty-six trillion years. He also taught that 6,600 years ago, the black nation gave birth to another wise scientist (considered God's agent) named Yakub (pronounced, "yah-koob," similar to the Hebrew pronunciation of Jacob. Many correlations were drawn between the character Yakub and the biblical Jew, Jacob, who is one of the forefathers of the nation of Israel). He started studying the "life germ" of man to try making a new creation (the doctrine of the new man, 2 Corinthians 5:17, "Therefore, if anyone is in Christ, he is a new creation") whom the twenty-four scientists had foretold 8,400 years before the birth of Mr. Yakub. In addition, the scientists were aware of his birth and work before he was born (there are always twenty-four black scientists present on the earth at all times whose job it is to receive divine revelation for the advancement of the black race. Of this presbytery of twenty-four, one sits to judge his fellows). Yakub was seen by the twenty-three scientists of the black nation, over 15,000 years ago. They predicted that in the year 8,400 (according to the calendar year of the black nation, before the world of the white race), this man Yakub would be born twenty miles from the present Holy City of Mecca, Arabia.

Now keep in mind as you continue to read this story about the history of the black nation and Mr. Yakub, that this is a legend. However, this is what was believed and taught by Elijah Muhammad and his followers.

At the time of his birth, the "divine ratio" of satisfaction and dissatisfaction of the people of the earth would be 70 percent satisfied, 30 percent dissatisfied. Mr. Yakub was born out of the 30 percent who were dissatisfied. Elijah Muhammad taught that Master Fard Muhammad had said to him, "When Yakub was six years old he was sitting down playing with two pieces of steel. He noticed the magnetic power in the steel attracting the other. He looked up at his uncle and said, "Uncle, when I get to be an old man I am going to make a people who shall rule you." His uncle said, "What will you make, something to make mischief and cause bloodshed in the land?" Yakub said, "Nevertheless, uncle, I know that which you do not know." It was at this moment that Yakub first came into the knowledge of just who he was, born to make trouble, break peace, kill and destroy his own people by fashioning an enemy of the black nation. This speaks to the magnetic power of attraction: the one attracting and drawing the other under its power. With this attraction, Yakub envisioned an unlikable human being, made to attract others, who could, with the knowledge of tricks and lies, rule the original black man until that nation could produce one greater and capable of overcoming this devil race with truth. And so we were taught that Yakub was the founder of the universal principle "unlike attracts and like repels."

Yakub began school at the age of four. His head was of an unusual size. When he had grown up the others referred to him as "the big-head scientist." At the age of eighteen he had finished all of the colleges and universities of his nation. In addition, he was seen preaching on the streets of Mecca, making converts. He made such an impression on the people that many began to follow him. He learned from studying "the germ of the black man" under the microscope, that there were two people in him, and that one was black, the other brown. He said if he could successfully separate the one from the other, he could graft the brown germ into its last stage, which would be white. With his wisdom, he discovered that he could make the white, which was the weaker of the black germ (which would be unalike), rule the black nation for a time.

With this new idea he went to work finding the necessary converts to begin grafting his new race of people. Mr. Yakub brought all his new converts together and told them his plan for making a new people who would rule for 6,000 years. He called the doctor first and said, "Doctor, let all the people come to you who want to marry, and if there come to you two real black ones, take a needle and get a little of their blood and go into your room and pretend to be examining it, to see whether their blood would mix. (It was the aim of Yakub to get rid of the black and he did.) Give them a certificate to take to the minister, warning the minister against marrying the couple because their blood does not mix. When there comes to you two browner ones, take a pretended blood test of them; but give them a certificate saying that they are eligible to marry."

Mr. Yakub was very strict on his laborers, death if one disobeyed. They did not know what Yakub had in mind until they were given their labor to do. He made his laborers, from the chief to the least, liars. The doctor lied about the blood of the two black people who wanted to marry; their blood did not mix. The brown and black could not be married, but only brown to brown. Yakub's aim was to kill and destroy the black nation. He ordered the nurses to kill all black babies that were born among his people, by pricking the brains with sharp needle as soon as the black child's head is out of the mother. If the mother is watching the nurse, then the nurse would lie and fool the mother to get possession of the child to murder it, by saying that she (the mother) gave birth to an angel child. And that she (the nurse) would like to take the baby to heaven, so when the mother dies, she would have a room with her child in heaven, for her baby was an angel. When there was a birth of a brown baby, the nurse would come and make a fuss over it. She was to tell the mother that she had given birth to a holy child and that she would nurse it for the next six weeks, for her child was going to be a great man (if it was a boy).

After the first two hundred years, Mr. Yakub had done away with the black babies, and all were brown. After another two hundred years, he had all yellow or red. And another two hundred years he had an all-pale, white race of people, which he called devils. Now Mr. Yakub only lived one hundred and fifty years, but prior to his death he gave instructions to his followers how to complete the process of making the white race. He gave his people guidance in the form of literature, instructing them what they should do and how to do it. He told them that when the evolution of the devil race was completed, the black race was to return to the Holy Land.

The twenty-three scientists predicted that when Yakub was born he would change civilization (the world) and produce a new race of people. The twenty-three scientists write and predict history, and the twenty-fourth sits as the judge. Their new people would be evil and deceiving, a race of devils. They would rule the original black nation for 6,000 years (from the nine thousandth year to the fifteen thousandth year). After that time, the original black nation would give birth to one whose wisdom, knowledge, and power would be infinite. One whom the world would recognize as being the greatest and mightiest God since the creation of the universe and who would destroy Yakub's world and restore the original nation, or ancient nation, into power to rule forever. Elijah Muhammad taught his followers that this mighty one is known under many names. He has no equal. He is referred to in the Bible as God Almighty, and in some places as Jehovah, the God of Gods, and the Lord of Lords. The Holy Qur'an refers to him as Allah, the one God; besides him, there is no God, and there is none like him, the Supreme Being. He is also referred to as the Christ, the second Jesus, and the Son of Man. He is none other than Master Fard Muhammad, God in person. We were taught that this was the savior and God of the black race. (We know that Jesus Christ is the only Savior of the world, or any race of people, but the NOI holds to a theology based entirely upon race). This history of Yakub can be found in the books written by Elijah Muhammad,

The True History of Master Fard Muhammad, and *Message to the Black Man in America.*

The Influence of Minister Louis Farrakhan

From 1981 to 1985 the name of the organization was changed. During this time the organization was putting itself forth as the American Muslim Mission. The imam, Warith Deen Muhammad, piloted his people to what is today a de-centralized, yet thriving society of Muslim Americans, with mosques and schools in every major city in America, and in parts of Canada and the Caribbean. By distancing the organization from the legend of Yakub and aligning its identity a bit closer to mainstream Islamic teaching, imam Muhammad garnered respect and acceptance for his branch of Islamic religion in the west that had not been previously known.

However, in January of 1977, Minister Louis Farrakhan could no longer tolerate these changes in the structure of the Nation of Islam. He met with Warith Deen Muhammad[‡] in Washington, D.C., and announced his withdrawal from the Muslim community. He opposed the disregard given the more mystical teaching of the Honorable Elijah Muhammad and what he considered to be the dismantling of the Nation of Islam.

After two years and seven months, Minister Louis Farrakhan began to rebuild the Nation of Islam. In May of 1979, he went public with his mission by launching *The Final Call* newspaper, naming the publication after the first official publication of the Nation of Islam, published in 1934.

Minister Farrakhan used many black organizations and the African-American churches to help expose the re-emerging Nation of Islam movement. On October 7, 1979, he gave public tribute to the Honorable Elijah Muhammad at the Medinah Temple in Chicago. The title of the event was the Second National Address to an Oppressed People, and it was sponsored by the National Conference of Black Lawyers Community College of Law. Standing with him were:

- Reverend Al Sampson of Southern Christian Leadership Conference, Chicago.
- Reverend Charles Koen, former member of the radical organization, the Black Egyptians of East St. Louis from 1968-1969. He then became co-pastor of Christian Hope Church, Chicago.
- Father George Clemens of Chicago.

In 1979, Minister Farrakhan began traveling all over the country speaking and drawing men and women into his emerging NOI. February 22, 1981, was a historic day for the rebuilding of the NOI. This was the first Savior's Day convention presided over by Minister Louis Farrakhan. Held in Chicago, the title of the convention was, A Savior is Born for the Black Men and Women of America. He declared in his speech:

> ...That the Most Honorable Elijah Muhammad is the modern day Jesus of the Bible and is physically alive! I know you think that Elijah Muhammad is dead, but I stand to proclaim to the world that He is alive, well, and in power... You evil conspirators thought you had killed Him. You damnable hypocrites rejoiced at what you perceived as His death. Now die in your rage, for Elijah is back! said the Minister.[7]

It is important to understand the impact that NOI has had on the African-American congregation (church) as a whole, and how Minister Louis Farrakhan targeted these churches. He literally used them as a springboard to promote the theology of the Nation of Islam. In fact, Minister Farrakhan made so many public appeals that it is easier for me to list some of his many speaking engagements, which were given in the African-American churches. Keep in mind that the message he brought was Black Nation Building in the name of Allah. When Minister Farrakhan uses the title *Christ,* he is not always referring to the Christ of the Bible. Many times, he is talking about Master Fard Muhammad or Elijah Muhammad, the Christ or Messiah of the NOI.

- August of 1981–Missionary Baptist Church, Chicago, Illinois. The subject was In Christ All Things Are Possible.
- December 20, 1981–Fuller Building, Chicago, Illinois. The subject was The Life of Jesus.
- March 14, 1982–Methodist Church, Chicago, Illinois. The subject was A Motherless Child in the Wilderness.
- April 13, 1983–Holy Angels Catholic Church, Buffalo, New York. The subject was The Protection of The Black Community.

In May of 1983, Minister Farrakhan began a thirteen-city tour on the theme, Christ's Imminent Return: He Makes All Things New, with the first stop being Bible-Way Baptist Church in Washington, D.C. Minister Farrakhan is not a Christian. His agenda was to gain the trust of the Christian church and to reach the black population for the Nation of Islam to which he was clearly dedicated.

In addition, Minister Farrakhan began to reach out to prominent black leaders and organizations. This list of his many speaking engagements included:

- January 19, 1980, Minister Farrakhan taught at the Black Woman's Forum held at the Ambassador Hotel in Oakland, California.
- November of 1983, at the National Association for the Advancement of Colored People (NAACP) gala in Washington, D.C., Minister Farrakhan delivered the keynote address.
- December of 1983, Minister Farrakhan traveled to Damascus and Syria with Rev. Jesse Jackson.
- January of 1984, Minister Farrakhan, Rev. Jesse Jackson, and some black clergy attended a White House briefing with former President Ronald Reagan and Vice President George Bush to announce the safe return of Navy Lieutenant Robert Goodman from Syria.
- On July 30, 1984, he addressed the National Press Club in Washington, D.C. with 4,200 distinguished journalists in attendance. The topic was Warn America that she faces Divine Chastisement from God if she does not Solve the four hundred-year-old Problem of Black people, with Justice.
- August, of 1984, Minister Farrakhan addressed the United Nations.

Reaching Out to Nations, 1986

- February 5, 1986, Minister Farrakhan began another world tour. He visited the Caribbean, Central and South America, Africa, and the Middle East.
- February 6, 1986, destination: Lagos, Nigeria.
- February 11, 1986, destination: Accra, Ghana. Topic was The Black People of America and Africa: Building a Bridge of Unity.
- February 12, his topic was Islam, Christianity, and Africa Tribal Religions. He also addressed the Ghanaian Army.

- March 16, 1986, Tripoli, Libya, address to the Second World Mathabah Conference of Third World Revolutionaries. He also introduced Colonel Muammar Ghadafi.
- May 5, 1986, destination: United Arab Emirates.

Minister Farrakhan's Travels from 1987 to 1996

It is apparent that Minister Farrakhan was successful in his attempts to network among prominent black leaders and gain their respect. I have no problem with his being a spokesperson for the struggles of African Americans, but he had a solemn commitment to the Nation of Islam and its Muslim theology that apparently went completely unchallenged by politicians and clergy alike. He was never held accountable for speaking in the name of Christ in the churches. Was it his charisma and mounting political affiliations that caused pastor after pastor to sell out the gospel of Jesus Christ? Were they hoping to use Minister Farrakhan as a springboard to open up the dialogue regarding the black experience in America to their congregations, bringing in a wolf in sheep's clothing, and suspending their own responsibilities for pastoral oversight? Whatever the attraction was, it was powerful and far reaching.

The Million Man March – A Line in the Sand

October 16, 1995 Declared a Holy Day

> Declaration: In the presence of God we humbly declare our earnest and sincere commitment to atone to God for our sins and for the sins of our people in our long struggle for liberation.

> As religious and spiritual leaders and ministers of faith to our people, we call upon all our people to repent, to atone, and reconcile ourselves to the God of our creation and salvation.
>
> We solemnly declare October 15, 1995, as a Holy Day of Atonement and Reconciliation.
>
> We call upon all our people to be in prayer and solidarity on this Holy Day. There is to be no work, no school, no sport or play, no entertainment, and nothing profane on this Holy Day. For those who are able, there should be fasting from sundown on the day before, until sundown on the day of this Holy Day.
>
> Let us all be in unity with God and with one another as we recommit and renew our determination to do God's will and seek justice, freedom, and empowerment for our people.[8]

Eighty religious leaders read this declaration together on September 19, 1995, at Rankin Chapel on Howard University campus in Washington, D.C. I personally believe that the Million Man March did a lot of good for the African American community. However, I know that God is not moved by our good works.

> There is none that doeth good, no, not one.
>
> —Romans 3:12 KJV

> For there is not a just man on earth who does good and does not sin.
>
> —Ecclesiastes 7:20 NKJV

What moves God is His purpose, not our plans.

> Many are the plans in a man's heart, but it is the LORD's purpose that prevails.
>
> —Proverbs 19:21 NIV

Minister Louis Farrakhan Calls for the One Million Man March

Minister Louis Farrakhan said that Allah (God) told him to call this march. He then asked Dr. Benjamin Chavis, an ordained minister of the gospel of our Lord Jesus Christ, to be the National Director for the Million Man March, which took place on October 16, 1995, in Washington D.C.

Minister Farrakhan was quoted in *The Final Call* newspaper, dated December 14, 1994:

> For 440 years the Black male has been the object of scorn, ridicule, and abuse, worse than that suffered by any people in the annals of history. The Black male is so destroyed, that Allah (God) Himself has to do today what He did in the beginning, and that is to declare His involvement in the process of the remaking of man. We, as students and followers of the Honorable Elijah Muhammad, are calling on all able-bodied Black men to set aside a day, October 16, 1995, for a historic March on Washington to declare to the Government of America and the world, that we are ready to take our place as the head of our families and our communities and that we, as Black men, are ready to shoulder the responsibility of being the maintainers of our women and children and the builders of our communities.
>
> There is enough unused and undeveloped talent in the Black male to build an entirely New World. The Almighty Allah (God) has declared that the time is ripe; and, that we must get up from our assigned place at the foot of the rulers of this world and show forth the Wisdom and

> Power of Allah (God) in doing something for ourselves. We must now show the world our resolve; for it is we, Black men, who cleared the underbrush, laid the tracks for the railroad, built the homes in the south for the slave master. It is we who plowed their fields, helped build their roads. It is we who fought in all of America's wars for a freedom that we have yet to enjoy.
>
> So, now the God of Justice has declared that it is time for us as Black men and as Christians, Muslims, Nationalists, Agnostics, young and old members of every fraternal, civic, and political organization to stand together as one to declare our right to justice and our right to determine the future of ourselves and our people.

The date of the march was scheduled for October 16, 1995—Yom Kippur, which is the most holy day of the Jewish calendar, the Day of Atonement. He attracted not only the attention of the Jewish community, but several liberal Jewish leaders marched in the rally. This date is also nine days after the birth date of Elijah Muhammad, October 7, which is celebrated by the NOI. This march would be symbolic of the works of Elijah Muhammad in the minds of the NOI faithful.

The Spirit of King Ahab

Minister Farrakhan has taught that Elijah Muhammad is the modern day Jesus and is physically alive. He called the Million Man March a fulfillment of what was written in the book of Ezekiel:

> That the dry bones would hear a word that would stimulate them, causing them to move, but there would be no spirit or breath in these bones to make them stand

> up. The son of man went back to his Sender pleading for more power to resurrect these bones and the Mighty God told the son of man to call on the winds and let them blow on these slain of God. When the winds began to blow on the bones, the scriptures said the bones stood up, an exceedingly great army.[9]

However, for the march to be successful, Minister Farrakhan needed the help of the African American clergy.

Likewise, King Ahab had to ask King Jehoshaphat for help. He knew that he could not defeat his enemy without the help of the man of God. I encourage you to read this very interesting story found in 2 Chronicles 18:1-34. King Ahab asked King Jehoshaphat to join forces with him against Ramoth-Gilead. King Jehoshaphat agreed. In the Living Bible it is paraphrased this way: "Why, of course!" King Jehoshaphat replied. "I'm with you all the way. My troops are at your command! However, let's check with the Lord first" (2 Chronicles 18:3b-4). But God never approved of King Jehoshaphat joining forces with King Ahab. Verse 5 reads: "So King Ahab summoned 400 of his heathen prophets and asked them, 'Shall we go to war with Ramoth-Gilead or not?' And they replied, 'Go ahead, for God will give you a great victory!'" The rest of the chapter points out that "a lying spirit" came out of the mouths of these prophets.

Doctor and Reverend Benjamin Chavis, the former executive director of the NAACP, an ordained minister in the United Church of Christ and former leader of the denomination's Commission for Racial Justice, joined the Nation of Islam, calling it a vehicle to resurrect black people.

On February 23, 1997, during the annual Savior's Day Conference that attracted six thousand people to the

University of Illinois campus in Chicago, Reverend Chavis announced:

> God has called me into the Nation of Islam and I have accepted God's call to the ministry of Islam. It was God, not man or woman, who called me into the Christian ministry. The God of Moses, Jesus, and Muhammad is the same God. I affirm the oneness of God and the oneness of humanity. It is God, not the forces of this world, and God only who discloses God's self today as Allah (God)."[10]

Dr. Chavis is now known as Dr. Benjamin F. (Chavis) Muhammad and Minister Benjamin Muhammad. To join the Nation of Islam, Chavis would have had to agree to a proclamation of faith that holds that Allah (God) appeared in the person of Master W. Fard Muhammad, July 1930, as the long-awaited Messiah of the Christians and the Mahid of the Muslims. Additionally, he would have to acknowledge that Elijah Muhammad is the messenger of Allah (God).

Defining Atonement and Reconciliation

The title given to the Million Man March was a Holy Day of Atonement and Reconciliation. As Director of the march, Dr. Chavis' first responsibility was to God, his Savior, Jesus Christ. As an ordained minister of the gospel, he should have known there is no atonement without the shedding of blood, and without atonement, there is no reconciling with God. How can anyone direct millions of men to a march without the proper understanding of true atonement and reconciliation? We must first make atonement (be in good standing in our relationship) with God before we can reconcile with each other. The keynote speaker must also have an understanding of the Jewish sacrificial system and the atoning blood of Jesus.

What do the words *atonement* and *reconciliation* mean? *Atonement* comes from the Hebrew word *kaphar,* which means, "to cover, cancel, cleanse, forgive, and purge." Reconciliation comes from the word *reconcile,* the English word meaning, "to cause to be friendly again; to bring back to harmony, to make peace." The Greek translation of reconciliation is: (a) *katallasso,* a verb, and (b) *katallage,* the noun form. This word comes from *kata* which means, "down," and *allaso* meaning, "to change or exchange." Thus *katallasso* means "to change from enmity or disharmony to friendship and harmony" or "to reconcile." For an example of its usage see Romans 5:10.

According to the Bible, there is no atonement apart from blood.

> And Aaron shall make atonement upon its horns once a year with the blood of the sin offering of *atonement*; once a year he shall make *atonement* upon it throughout your generations. It is most holy to the Lord.
>
> —Exodus 30:10 NKJV, emphasis added

The Holy Day of Atonement is a very important day for Christians. It is the tenth day of the seventh month ("Tishri" September-October / Jewish calendar). The Jews call it Yom Kippur. In Hebrew *Yom* means "day" (marked from sunset to sunset) and *Kippur* means, "to pardon, or condone." The observance of the Day of Atonement originates with Moses.

> And the Lord spoke to Moses, saying: "Also the tenth day of this seventh month shall be the Day of Atonement. It shall be a holy convocation for you; you shall afflict your souls, and offer an offering made by fire to the LORD. And you shall do no work on that same day, for it is the

> Day of Atonement, to make atonement for you before the LORD your God.
>
> —Leviticus 23:26-28 NKJV

On the Day of Atonement, once a year, the high priest would enter the Most Holy Place of the Tabernacle to offer ceremonial sacrifices for the forgiveness of the sins of the people (Hebrews 9:7). That ancient observance was a direct fore-picture of Jesus Christ, our High Priest (Hebrews 9:11), who after his sacrifice entered the very throne room of God the Father in heaven to make atonement for all humanity (Hebrews 9:11-12). The Day of Atonement also involved the Azazel goat, or scapegoat, which was taken out into the wilderness after having had all of the sins of the Israelites ceremonially placed upon it (Leviticus 16:10, 21-22). The scapegoat symbolized the condemnation of Satan for the sins of all humanity, and his being put away in an eternal wilderness from which he will never return (see Revelation 20:10). The sending of the Azazel goat out into the wilderness by the Levitical high priest after he returned from inside the Most Holy Place of the Tabernacle is a ceremonial preview of Jesus Christ sending Satan into the abyss, which will be done after Jesus' return.

The Day of Atonement signifies three most vital aspects of Christianity:

1. Willing repentance on the part of those to be saved.
2. The completed sacrifice of Jesus Christ formally presented to God the Father as atonement for the sins of humanity.
3. The final guilty verdict upon Satan as the source of all evil, and the sentencing of him to eternity in the abyss.

According to the historic context of atonement and reconciliation, Minister Louis Farrakhan would not qualify to be a keynote speaker on such a topic.

The March Begins

The march officially started at 5:00 A.M. with the calling of the *Adhan* (the Muslim call to prayer). It was called in a loud voice by the *muazzin* (caller). The muazzin stands facing the *qibla* (the (Ka'ba / black stone) in Mecca, Saudi Arabia.

The Muslim prayer went forth in Arabic. They declared:

In Quranic Arabic	**Translated to English**
Allahu Akbar, Allahu Akbar, Allahu Akbar, Allahu Akbar	Allah is the greatest (repeated four times)
Ash hadu an la ilaha illa llah Rasul-llah Ash hadu an la ilaha illa llah	I bear witness that Muhammad is the Messenger of Allah (repeated twice)
Hayya 'ala-s-sala, Hayya 'ala-s-sala	Come to prayer (repeated twice)
Hayya 'ala-l-falah, Hayya 'ala-l-falah	Come to success (repeated twice)
Allahu Akbar, Allahu Akbar	Allah is the greatest (repeated twice)
La illaha illa-lah	Nothing deserves to be worshipped except Allah

After this prayer, the spirit of Islam was released in the atmosphere over the march. What is the spirit of Islam? It bears witness that there is no God but Allah and that

Muhammad is his last and greatest prophet. There will be no more prophets after him; he is the seal of the prophets. The spirit of Islam rejects Jesus as the Son of God. Furthermore, it is a sin against Allah for a Muslim to claim that Jesus was God in the flesh; it is enmity with Allah. The spirit of Islam is an antichrist spirit.

> Who is a liar but he who denies that Jesus is the Christ? He is antichrist who denies the Father and the Son.
>
> —1 John 2:22 NKJV

> Beloved, do not believe every spirit, but test the spirits, whether they are of God; because many false prophets have gone out into the world. By this, you know the Spirit of God: Every spirit that confesses that Jesus Christ has come in the flesh is of God, and every spirit that does not confess that Jesus Christ has come in the flesh is not of God. And this is the spirit of the Antichrist, which you have heard was coming, and is now already in the world.
>
> —1 John 4:1-3 NKJV

Later that morning both Christian and Muslim ministers worked together to establish the tone of the march. However, the Muslims of the Nation of Islam had already claimed the day for Allah.

Rev. Al Sampson of Fernwood United Methodist Church, Chicago, addressed the assembled crowd. "I stand here today to ask your permission to make a motion. I make a motion that we accept Minister Louis Farrakhan as our leader all over the world for black men, for generations yet unborn, that he be our leader today, yesterday, and tomorrow."[11]

That is an outrageous statement. Was he attempting to speak for the entire Methodist Church? I highly doubt he had such authority.

Minister Farrakhan began his speech:

> In the name of Allah, the beneficent, the merciful. We thank Him for his prophets, and the scriptures which they brought. We thank him for Moses and the Torah. We thank him for Jesus and the Gospel. We thank him for Muhammad and the Quran. Peace be upon these worthy servants of Allah.
>
> I am so grateful to Allah for his intervention in our affairs…[here Minister Farrakhan makes it very clear who the God of Nation of Islam is and that he came in the person of Master Fard Muhammad the Great Mahdi (a divinely-guided Messiah), one for which most of the Muslim world is waiting. As I have stated before, the Nation of Islam believes that Fard Muhammad is God in the flesh and the Messiah (a Jesus) in person.]… who came among us and raised from among us a divine leader, teacher and guide, his messenger to us the Most Honorable Elijah Muhammad."[12]

One of the most famous parts of his speech that day was about the A-tone. He taught the following to the crowd assembled in the mall at the Washington Monument:

> The first four letters of the word form the foundation; a-t-o-n…*a-ton, a-ton*. Since this obelisk in front of us is representative of Egypt. In the 18th dynasty, a Pharaoh named Akhen-aton, was the first man of this history period to destroy the pantheon of many gods and bring the people to the worship of one god. And that one god was symbolized by a sun disk with 19 rays coming out of that sun with hands holding the Egyptian Ankh—the cross of life. A-ton. The name for the one god in ancient Egypt. A-ton, the one god. 19 rays. Look at your scripture. ...Black man, the a-ton represents the one

> God. In the Koran, Muhammad is called a light-giving son. So if you look at the aton, add an "e" to it, and separate the "a" from the next four letters and you get the word 'atone'.
>
> Atone means sound. And "a", the first letter of the alphabet and the first letter of the numerical system is one. So "a" equals one. So "a" sound means when you hear the "a" tone, you will hear the right sound. And when you hear the right sound from the one God calling you to divine life, you will respond. So what is the "a" tone? In music, "a" equals 440 vibrations. How long have we been in America? Four hundred and forty years.
>
> Well, in the 440th year, from the one God, the aton, will come the "a" tone and all of us got to tune up our lives by the sound of the "a" tone. Because we've got to atone for all that we have done wrong. And when you atone, if you take the "t" and couple it with the "a" and hyphenate it, you get at-one. So when you atone you become at-one. At one with who? The aton or the one God. Because you heard the "a" tone and you tuned up your life and now you're ready to make a new beginning."[13]

The above quoted dissertation has nothing to do with the biblical understanding of atoning and reconciling to God. It is a manipulation of words and a titillation of supposed *hidden wisdom*. Furthermore, it does absolutely nothing to establish the spiritual authority of the Nation of Islam.

Hell is real, and unless we individually repent of our sins, and accept what Christ accomplished on the cross, we will experience eternal death for rejecting the authority of the gospel of Jesus Christ.

> Jesus said, "I am the way, the truth and the life. No one comes to the father except through Me."
>
> —John 14:6 NKJV

International Impact

On July 6, 1997, the Nation of Islam, in conjunction with the World Islamic People's Leadership, hosted the International Islamic Conference at the McCormick Center Grand Auditorium, Chicago, Illinois. The theme of the conference was A Call for Peace in the 21st Century.

During this conference, Minister Farrakhan was crowned imam of the Islamic World by the Grand Sheikh (elder, Islamic scholar) of Egypt, Grand Sheikh of Ghana, Grand Sheikh of Nigeria, and the Vice President of Al-Azhar University, Cairo, Egypt, as well as many other world Islamic leaders. This is an unusual honor in the Islamic world. Al-Azhar University is one of the oldest operating universities. Al-Azhar pays special attention to the Quranic Sciences and traditions of the Prophet Muhammad. It is celebrated as one of, if not the best, Islamic academic institutions and universities in the world.

The subject for Farrakhan's speech that day was taken from the Qur'an, chapter 103 (Sura 103) entitled, Time through the Ages.

> As Muslims we have been the most divided by this century of war. As the superpowers fought, the Caesars of the world have asked Muslims again and again and again to do battle against their Muslim brothers in the great chess game that they have played....

In addition, Farrahkan stated that Islam accepts all of the prophets in the Torah and the prophet Jesus of the gospel. He said that Islam may be the youngest religion, but it is the best because Islam has come when all else has failed. He stated:

> "Islam is the best religion, and Muhammad, peace be upon him, is the last and greatest prophet of Allah (God), and the Holy Qur'an is the last revelation from Allah (God)," Minister Farrakhan said.[14]

Farrakhan went on to explain to the Islamic world leaders why Elijah Muhammad taught the Muslims of the NOI the way he did and why Master Fard Muhammad brought in Islam and taught the way he did. In essence, he said that Master Fard Muhammad and the Honorable Elijah Muhammad ushered in a new era for Islam; consequently Farrakhan called for unity in the Islamic world.

That day, Muslims of the world saw Minister Farrakhan call and attract over one million black men to the capital of the Untied States. They saw many Christian leaders submit to the leadership of a Muslim leader. Therefore, this International Islamic Conference was comparable in spiritual magnitude to what the Million Man March was in terms of physical magnitude.

The Church in Confusion

From 1988-1996, I had been traveling throughout the United States sharing my testimony and teaching Christians how to reach out to Muslims. In 1994, one year before the Million Man March, I was ministering at a conference and conducting a workshop on Orthodox Islam, Nation of Islam, and the Five Percenters. A pastor asked me to explain whether or not it would be right to take his members to support the Million Man March, because he had already explained to his congregation his support of

Minister Farrakhan and the march. I told him that if he went to evangelize and hand out literature on the gospel that would be great. However, if he told his congregation about his support of the march without explaining his disagreement with the *theology* of Minister Farrakhan, then he would be misleading his people. I will never forget his words: "I can't do that. I already told my people how I feel about this march."

There were other pastors in this workshop who were also preparing their people for the march. Many of them were willing to cancel their plans, but in the end, approximately eighty-five percent of the men who participated in the march were identified with the Christian church!

After the March

"Hey, brother." I turned and there stood a tall, young, handsome man. He wore a beige suit, white shirt, and a brown bowtie. He had in his hands the Muslim newspaper, *The Final Call,* and some handouts. "I would like to talk to you for a moment," he stated with boldness. "My name is Brother Muhammad, I want to invite you to the community forum we are having at the local church." He then handed me one of the handouts he was holding, and I began to read it. It was an influential church within the Asbury Park, New Jersey, community that was hosting this forum. The topics were "Losing Our Black Men to Drugs and Crimes," "Taking Our Community Back." Leaders from all over the community were invited—pastors, teachers, police officers, the mayor's office. The invited guest speaker was a top leader and representative of Minister Louis Farrakhan of the NOI. I decided to attend this meeting to observe.

As I entered the church along with others, we had to submit to a security search, how well I knew about this. As a former member of the Fruit of Islam (FOI), the military unit of the NOI, I had conducted many of their searches. I stood there wondering if that FOI knew what he was doing.

I entered the sanctuary and immediately noticed that the place was set up like a mosque. The men sat on one side of the church and the women on the other. The men of the FOI were sitting in chairs in front of the sanctuary, facing the audience. The two FOI were sitting in an upright position, looking fully alert–it is called being on your post. You could see that the Muslims were in charge of this meeting.

The meeting began with the Muslim's opening salutation by Minister Muhammad, who stated, "In the name of Allah, the beneficent, the merciful, to whom praise is due forever, the Lord of all the worlds. Who came in the person of Master Fard Muhammad. The God who raised in our midst the exalted Christ, the Most Honorable Elijah Muhammad. We also thank him for our divine guide the Most Honorable Minister Louis Farrakhan."

Each community leader who was part of the panel had five minutes to share on the two topics. They all acknowledged the presence of the members of the NOI in the community and the contributions they were making in the area of transforming the lives of drug addicts and criminals.

Now it was time for the host pastor to share and introduce the guest speaker. The pastor jumped out of his seat, took the microphone, and said in Arabic, "As-Salaam-Alaikum" (peace be unto you) and the audience responded, "Wa-Alaikum-Salaam"(unto you be peace). The pastor stated "We have invited the Muslims here, because they have the answers. They have demonstrated they can do what the church has failed to do. They are going into the youth correctional facilities and prisons and transforming lives of men. Their men are coming out of these institutions, shining and being productive citizens. I believe the Muslims can take back our communities."

The Muslim minister then stood up and began to teach that Elijah Muhammad is like a Jesus and that the Nation of Islam has the answers to the problems in our communities. He taught that Islam can give the black man freedom, justice, and equality. He said that if we support Minister Farrakhan and the program of the Honorable Elijah Muhammad, the problems of the black community would be solved.

Ironically, the pastor stood in the pulpit after the Muslim minister had finished and agreed that the Muslims of the NOI had the answers regarding freedom, justice, and equality. This gave the Muslim minister a great opportunity to seize the moment. He stood in the pulpit again and gave an open invitation to anyone who wanted to join the NOI. In other words, he gave an altar call to Islam, right in the church! Jesus said,

> I am the way, the truth and the life...And you shall know the truth, and the truth shall make you free...The thief does not come except to steal, and to kill, and to destroy. I have come that they may have life, and that they may have it more abundantly.
>
> —John 14:6, 8:32; 10:10 NKJV

I have seen this same scenery repeated all over this nation. Pastors are inviting and giving up their pulpits to ministers of the NOI. I have seen some pastors take their whole congregations to the mosque, putting their people under the teaching of Minister Farrakhan.

My fellow ministers in the gospel, the Bible is the Word of God. The gospel is the Good News. The answer to all of our problems is in the Word, not external to the Word. Let us stop looking outside of the body of Christ to solve our problems.

CHAPTER THREE

My Message to the Churches

TODAY WHEN I visit the churches, I let them know why it is that so many African Americans get involved in the Nation of Islam, as well as how racism in the church made room for the movement.

One of the stories I like to tell is about my days as a freshman in high school. My parents had just bought a home in an all-white neighborhood. Ironically, our neighbor from that time was now my Sunday school teacher. There was also a pair of twins in the neighborhood, a boy and girl, who were the same age as my twin sister and me. We were friends and attended the same school about a mile from our home. We had to walk to school every day, yet our neighbors were driven to school by their parents. I do not remember ever receiving a ride. Nor can I remember having been in their home.

When I visited an all-white church, there was much to share about my involvement in the Nation of Islam. The perspective I presented was eye-opening for many. They didn't know that the NOI taught that the Bible was written by the white man to benefit him and to enslave and suppress blacks. I explained that when the black man was brought to America, our culture, our language, and our heritage were taken away. The culture today is slowly changing, but for decades following the Emancipation Proclamation, the white race has been portrayed in the media, schools, books, and magazines as the standard of beauty and intelligence.

Prejudices persist. Definitions for the word "black" in the dictionary are listed as lacking hue and brightness; belonging to an ethnic group of African descent; soiled, stained, gloomy, dismal, sullen or hostile, evil or wicked; indicating disgrace. On the other hand, the word "white" is defined as the color of pure snow; belonging to a people having light skin; morally pure, without malice; politically ultraconservative. We are talking about the power of words and labels.

The result in our psyches was and still is a superiority complex in whites and an inferiority complex in blacks. For years many black people have justified this divide within themselves. I still hear, "What would happen to your subconscious mind if for four hundred years you sat in church and looked at a picture of a white Jesus as your Savior?"

However, the real issue is much bigger. We cannot deny that Jesus was a Jew. We need to remember that Jesus required his followers to live in a way that transcended race and religious and national loyalties, just as he did. That is something the church still has trouble doing to this day. We can't fix the problem by changing the color of Jesus' skin, as some congregations have done. Our problem lies in discerning the gospel of Jesus Christ and living it!

Once I was speaking at a large black church in Newark, New Jersey, on the subject of superiority and inferiority.

The senior pastor was white. After I finished ministering, he took the microphone and began crying. I said to him, "What is wrong, why are you crying?"

"My wife and I came into this neighborhood thinking that these people needed us. I did not realize until now that subconsciously I have a superiority complex. The Holy Spirit convicted me as you were speaking. I repent now for that spirit of offence."

This is where we need to start when discerning the gospel of Jesus Christ. We need to make it very personal.

The African American church has also bought into this spirit of racism. For instance, we participate in the celebration of black history month in February. (There is nothing inherently wrong with this.) Many years ago when I was a youth leader, one of our youth members wanted to share during our Sunday worship service about how Malcolm X was a great African American leader. I agreed with her that he fought against the oppression of black people. However, I had to challenge her to embrace some realities. I asked her, "Did Malcolm X advance the kingdom of God? Did he make all men brothers and give them the way to live in peace?"

She replied, "Malcolm X did not know our God, and he was not about the kingdom of God. He did not accept the revelation of Jesus Christ as Lord and Savior; Prophet Muhammad was his example and teacher, and Allah was his God."

It is time for us to realize that the color of our skin does not matter, but our ultimate spiritual allegiance and destiny in our day-to-day matters certainly does!

Christ came to destroy the works of the enemy; racism is the work of the devil. There is no superior race. The body of Christ must get serious about overcoming racism in the church. Jesus didn't create a white church or black church or any other ethnic church. Nor did he create a denominational church. We are many members of one body (1 Corinthians 12:12-27). We are one church, the church of the Lord Jesus Christ. Jesus Christ is the salvation and empowerment of all people, highlighting the needs of the oppressed, but regarding no one's race, religious creed, or nation of origin.

The Issue of Identity

While growing up I had been very confused. My race had been called niggers, Negroes, colored people, black people, Afro-American, African American, but I did not know who I was. At the time, the Nation of Islam gave me a sense of identity. (Praise be to God I now know my identity.) I know my true identity is not in my skin color or my African heritage or even as an American. My true identity is a child of God in Christ Jesus.

> There is neither Jew nor Greek, there is neither slave nor free, there is neither male nor female; for you are all one in Christ Jesus.
>
> —Galatians 3:38 NKJV

As I began to study the teaching and the history of the NOI, I read *Message to the Black Man in America* by the Honorable Elijah Muhammad (as he was called by his followers), and anything else I could about the Nation of Islam. There were several key doctrines put forth by NOI that were especially attractive, specifically the Approaches to Islam Among African Americans and the Black Muslim Experience and Expression in the United States. I was certainly not alone in finding solace in a black race-based worldview. The black experience in America began with the tragedy of slavery. Carl Ellis—theologian, author, and professor, whom I have had the privilege of meeting—and his colleague Adam Edgerly provide a nice synopsis of the dynamics of this experience:

> The African American experience and expression in the United States began when the slaves from Africa were brought to America. The African slaves saw themselves as strangers in a land that was not theirs. Some of the slaves identified with the children of Israel in Egyptian bondage and saw the hand of God at work in terms of their hope of deliverance from slavery. This theology addressed the issues of survival, refuge, and resistance to oppression. They were caught in a theological paradigm called "Exodus."
>
> In the ante-bellum North where slavery had died out, the theological paradigm was the Exile. The Freedmen saw the hand of God at work in terms of a special calling they sensed to bring the gospel of Christ to the rest of the African descents living in the South. Had it fully developed, this theology would have addressed the issues of dignity, African identity, and global significance.
>
> With the official end of slavery in 1865, the former slaves were devastated and confused about their identity in the economy of God. Yet the indigenous African-American church experienced explosive growth. A major contributing factor was the fact that the church in the North and the South adequately addressed the need for a true identity. This was achieved when the church became actively involved in cultural and economic development in the United States and in missions, particularly in Africa.
>
> However, three events radically altered the theological direction of the African American church.

1. The end of the post-Civil War reconstruction in the South in 1877.
2. The Industrial Revolution in the North.
3. The consolidation of European colonialism in Africa as the result of the Congress of Berlin (1878) and the Conference of Berlin (1884-1885).

With the end of reconstruction in the South, the former slaves were subject to racist terrorism and intimidation as white supremacy was re-established. Concurrent with the Industrial Revolution in the North was a massive wave of European immigration. This led to the rise of the white-only trade unions, resulting in the elimination of African American from the skilled labor force. The consolidation of colonialism in Africa further decimated the mission's movement of the African American church.

These traumas forced the church to abandon the Pan-African approach to ministry and revert to the old survival approach, which had emerged in the context of slavery. This created a theological vacuum in the areas of dignity, African identity, and global significance.

Several non-Christian attempts were made to fill this vacuum. Among them:

1. The NAACP, founded in 1909 by W. E. B. Dubois, an advocate of solidarity through education.
2. A few black Jewish sects.
3. Marcus Garvey and the United Negro Improvement Association (UMIA, established 1914).
4. Several black nationalist oriented Islam sects.

The first group that tried to fill this vacuum was the Muslim sect Moorish Science Temple Divine and National Movement of North America. In 1913 Timothy Drew, known by his followers as Prophet Noble Drew Ali,

> founded the Canaanite Temple in Newark, New Jersey. Drew Ali developed the Koran of the Moorish Holy Temple of Science and taught that Allah had ordained him as his prophet to the dark people of America. Ali stated that Negro and black signified death and colored signified something painted. Therefore, the terms Asiatic, Moor or Moorish-American must be used. Ali taught that salvation could be found by discovering national origin and refusing to be called names such as Negro, black, colored, or Ethiopian. Even though Noble Drew Ali died in 1929, the Moorish Science Temple of America is still functioning all over America.
>
> The second African American Muslim sect was the Nation of Islam. It was originally called the Lost Found Nation of Islam, founded by Fard Muhammad in 1930. Allah (God), revealed himself in the person of Master Fard Muhammad. He came to America to show that he alone had the power to resurrect that which had been destroyed. He first came to America in 1910 and studied the cultural differences of blacks and white Americans. He even lived with a white family and attended a college on the west coast. Mr. Fard said he came seeking that which was lost, and restore the black nation back to its original glory. He said he came to fulfill the original promise made to Abraham."[15]

You can see why many African Americans are still wrestling with the issue of identity. As a people group, they still suffer trauma from being sold into slavery in a foreign land. Their history is barely two hundred years behind us,

I want to challenge you to look beyond the temporal quagmire that slavery has brought upon us. No amount of money or land is going to correct the injustices. It is impossible for us to raise the dead or erase the past. The courts cannot put a dollar amount upon a human life. We need to embrace the truth that the issue of identity goes beyond skin color or family of origin. The question of a person's identity, regardless of experience and circumstance, is best resolved through a personal spirituality.

The NOI offered an element of spirituality, but its theology was based upon "sandy soil." The NOI proclaims a theology based upon an economy of race instead of the rock solid foundation of compassion and forgiveness found in Jesus Christ. From a Christian perspective, we are challenged to forgive every day. We are challenged *not* to see the deck stacked against us, but to believe in and seek equal opportunity for expression. Prejudice is still alive and well in our corporations, communities, and churches. There is still much work to be done socially and psychologically in order to bring understanding and healing. And every American is responsible before God to do his or her part to facilitate reconciliation. The Christian community is called to a communion with one another. We are our brother's keeper. No one can demand restitution, but we can continue calling attention to the need for justice by acknowledging the reality of the impact a black-versus-white system still has upon us.

The pain of prejudice still throbs in our generation—only the six generations after the Emancipation Proclamation—that so easily obscures the vision of a legitimate path to healing. Counterfeit communities and sects that take on the role of the victim on behalf of everyone and set up cultures of isolation or exclusivity are simply the paths of least resistance.

The truth is there are no shortcuts for the healing process. The hard work has to be done first on the individual level (I am speaking spiritually) and then in the wider social circle of our communities and governments.

Though we may have come far in terms of legislation (equal opportunity employment for example), grace and peace do not come through the law. Real peace and real peacemaking come by accepting the free gift of one's legitimate and ultimate identity within the body of Christ. Our Lord Jesus Christ demonstrated this when he preached about the freedom found in the kingdom of God. This is the true brotherhood of man, perhaps best exemplified in our generation through the life and legacy of Dr. Martin Luther King, Jr.

There is a saying: You cannot take a man down and not fall with him. Jesus said it this way: "Love your enemies." One of the paradigms of the gospel is that our healing is bound up in the healing of our enemies, not in their demise. This is an essential and universal spiritual key that is inextricably linked to issues of identity. It is sublime and often overlooked. It is neither a flashy political solution nor a show of superior intelligence or force. It is simple humility before an Almighty God who demands that we approach him on level ground with one another, or not at all.

> First be reconciled to your brother, then come and offer your gift.
>
> —Matthew 5:24 NKJV

> And behold, a certain lawyer stood up and tested Him [Jesus], saying, "Teacher, what shall I do to inherit eternal life?" He [Jesus] said to him, "What is written in the law? What is your reading of it?" So he answered and said, "You shall love the LORD your God with all your heart, with all your soul, with all your strength, and with all your mind,' and `your neighbor as yourself.'" And He said to him, "You have answered rightly; do this and you will

> live." But he, wanting to justify himself, said to Jesus, "And who is my neighbor?"
>
> —Luke 10:25-29 NKJV

Jesus proceeded to tell the man a story that places compassion above race, religion, and social caste—the story of the Good Samaritan. It is only in finding our identity as a child of God and discovering that our neighbor is our equal that we find the strength and courage for universal reconciliation. Peace on earth is only made possible by the gospel of our Lord Jesus Christ.

No matter the color of our skin or our experience of injustice or political power, the answers we seek are found in the one thing that levels the playing field for all—forgiveness. I truly believe that one day every knee will be made to bow before the wisdom and majesty of our Lord Jesus Christ.

The Problem with Affinity; Lacking Discernment

On June 13, 1993, Rev. Dr. Hycel B. Taylor, pastor of Second Baptist Church in Evanston, Illinois, was the guest speaker at the Nation of Islam Mosque in Chicago. His message was titled, What do Black Christians and Black Muslims Have in Common? Here are some quotes from an article that appeared in *The Final Call* newspaper.

> To the delight of the cheering audience, Rev. Taylor answered the question smiling broadly. "Obviously, the first thing we have in common is that we are Black." But more than that he said, "Black people must learn to not let names and titles separate them from one another. "Allah" only means God and "Islam" simply means to "submit," Rev. Taylor explained.[16]

> Rev. Taylor began in prayer. He recited in English the Al-Fatiha, or opening chapter of the Qur'an, which is the most repeated Muslim prayer. "There was a time when I wouldn't have entertained (the thought of) attending this kind of meeting. But we have come of age," Rev. Taylor said.[17]
>
> I find an affinity with your spirit," he said. "I make no apology for my desire at all times to stand with a brother who is fighting for our people.[18]

Many African American pastors agree with Rev. Taylor and have an affinity of spirit with Minister Farrakhan and his work. The problem I have is these zealous pastors believe that the God of the Nation of Islam and the God of the Bible are one and the same. I pray that all African American pastors who agree with the statements of Rev. Taylor would purchase a copy of *The Final Call* newspaper. On the last page there is a long-standing declaration that runs with every issue titled, "What The Muslims Want and What The Muslims Believe." Under the section What The Muslims Believe, you will find the following beliefs:

We believe in the One God whose proper name is Allah.[19]

- We believe that Allah (God) appeared in the person of Master W. Fard Muhammad, July 1930, the long-awaited "Messiah" of the Christians and the "Mahdi" of the Muslims.[20] (That explains why Minister Farrakhan so easily interchanged his use of the title Christ to fool pastors into thinking he was talking about Jesus Christ, when in fact he stood to proclaim the gospel of his own Master W. Fard Muhammad.)

- We believe in the truth of the Bible, but we believe that it has been tampered with and must be reinterpreted so that mankind will not be snared by the falsehoods that have been added to it.[21] [Belief number three plays to fear, conspiracy, suspicion, and prejudice – all works of Satan. Furthermore, this sets up the Nation of Islam as the final authority regarding the interpretation of Scripture, completely abdicating the teaching ministry of the Holy Spirit, which Jesus promised to His disciples in John 14:16, 26 and 17:13.]
- We believe further and lastly that Allah is God and besides *him* there is no God, and He will bring about a universal government of peace wherein we all can live in peace together."[22] (Belief twelve does not agree with the testimony of the Bible. Allah is not the God of Abraham, Isaac, and Jacob. Further, it does not identify the Messiah of the New Testament. I write this out of love: we Christians, followers of Jesus, the Christ, the Messiah, do not serve or worship the same God as do Minister Farrakhan and The Nation of Islam.)

The Testimony of Sacred Scripture

What does the Bible say about Jesus' deity? Does the Bible—the earliest and most historically reliable source of God's recorded Word—say Jesus is God? What does it tell us about him and his identity? Some scriptures go back seven hundred years before the life of Christ, such as the book of Isaiah.

> Therefore the Lord Himself will give you a sign: Behold, the virgin shall conceive and bear a Son, and shall call His name Immanuel.
>
> —Isaiah 7:14 NKJV

Immanuel literally means, "God with (among) us." The prophet Isaiah is quoted later in Matthew 1:23: "Behold, the virgin shall be with child, and bear a Son, and they shall call His name Immanuel," which is translated, "God with us."

Isaiah also foretold that the Messiah would be born a human son but have a higher nature.

> For unto us a Child is born, Unto us a Son is given; And the government will be upon His shoulder. And His name will be called Wonderful, Counselor, Mighty God, Everlasting, Father, Prince of Peace.
>
> —Isaiah 9:6 NKJV

This was a radical statement coming from a monotheistic Jewish prophet, especially calling a human being Mighty God, but one that God fulfilled centuries later in Jesus Christ.

A couple hundred years after Isaiah, Daniel also foretold of the Messiah's divine nature.

> I was watching in the night visions, And behold, One like the Son of Man, Coming with the clouds of heaven! He came to the Ancient of Days, And they brought Him near before Him. Then to Him was given dominion and glory and a kingdom. That all people, nations, and languages should serve Him. His dominion is an everlasting dominion, which shall not pass away, and His kingdom the one which shall not be destroyed.
>
> —Daniel 7:13-14 NKJV

Son of Man was the primary title Jesus used for himself. This passage shows a clear and strong identification of the Son of Man with deity. In addition, the Gospel of Mark included the unmistakable phrase, "coming on the clouds of heaven," with which Jesus identified.

> Jesus said, I am, And you will see the Son of Man sitting at the right hand of the Power, and coming with the clouds of heaven.
>
> —Mark 14:62 NKJV

> Jesus said, "I and My Father are one"... Then the Jewish leaders picked up stones to try to kill him. Jesus asked them, "Many good works I have shown you from my Father. For which of those works do you stone me?"... They answered "For a good work we do not stone you, but for blasphemy, and because You, being a Man, make Yourself God.
>
> —John 10:30-33 NKJV

Finally Jesus told Thomas, who was an eyewitness of the resurrection of Christ, to look at Jesus' hands and put his hands in his side; to not be unbelieving, but believing (John 20:27).

> In the beginning was the Word, and the Word was with God, and the Word was God... The Word became flesh and made his dwelling among us.
>
> —John 1:1,14 NIV

> He is the image of the invisible God, the firstborn over all creation. For by Him all things were created that are in heaven and that are on earth, visible and invisible, whether thrones or dominions or principalities or power. All things were created through Him and for Him. And He is the head of the body, the church, who is the beginning,

> the firstborn from the dead, that in all things He may have the preeminence.
>
> —Colossians 1:15, 18 NKJV

The Bible also says that in Jesus dwells all the fullness of the Godhead bodily (Colossians 2:9) and that Jesus is the brightness of God's glory and the express image of His person (Hebrews 1:3). These scriptures declare the perfection and divinity of Jesus Christ, not Fard Muhammad.

There is only one Messiah capable of the perfection required to unite all mankind, our Lord Jesus Christ. The very name of Jesus Christ carries heavenly power. The Godhead itself, revealed in the mystery of Father, Son, and Holy Spirit, is capable of defending and declaring his own Name. Our feeble words *he* and *his* are not sufficient to declare the glory of the one true God, beyond male and female, who is so pre-eminent that He can only be brought near to us in mystery.

God came to earth in the person of Jesus Christ to accomplish a very specific task, one that only the Godhead could accomplish. He did not send a mere man or a prophet confined to the culture and experience of his own age to do his saving work; he accomplished it himself on the cross, which was for all people, everywhere. The simple message of a suffering servant is sufficient to save a soul from any culture and walk of life ever created.

The god of Islam and the god of Minister Farrakhan are not the same God that we as Christians (followers of Christ) serve. We, as followers of Christ, the Messiah, cannot accept Prophet Muhammad Ibn Abdullah, who was born in Mecca, Arabia, around 570 A.D., as the last prophet of the Almighty God. Nor can we accept Elijah Muhammad as the messenger of this Almighty God. Elijah Muhammad was not entrusted with a gospel to save all mankind. He was not given the divine power to accomplish salvation for all mankind. In addition, neither is Fard Muhammad who he claims to be—God in person coming as a savior to the entire world.

Spirit of the Antichrist

Throughout the Bible there are warnings to the faithful to watch out for false leaders who do not believe that Jesus Christ came to earth as a human being. These false leaders stand against the testimony of God's Word concerning Jesus Christ. False leaders also stand against the reality of recorded history, usually offering some "hidden knowledge" (again, conspiracy thinking).

Those who purport hidden knowledge are akin to those who deny the Holocaust, deny that man has walked on the moon, or insist that the world is flat. However, those who deny that Jesus Christ was God in the flesh, the Savior of the world, also deny the testimony of the Holy Spirit. I am not saying that some of these leaders do not have good ideals, but none of them qualifies to die for the sins of the world. They cannot bring us back into full relationship with God. Anyone who does not believe that Jesus Christ came to earth from heaven, born in human flesh, operates out of an antichrist spirit.

> For many deceivers have gone out into the world who do not confess Jesus Christ as coming in the flesh. This is a deceiver and an antichrist.
>
> —2 John 1:7 NKJV

The Bible clearly instructs us regarding the revelation of the one true God. It tells us not to believe everything we hear just because someone says it is a message from God.

The Bible tells us to test what a person says first to see if it is really from God. The way to find out if the message is from the Holy Spirit is to ask, *Does it agree that Jesus Christ, God's Son, actually became man with a human body*? If so, then the message is from God. If not, the message is not from God but from one who is against Christ and his gospel. This is the Antichrist or the spirit of Antichrist. Their belief is enmity against the Spirit and the grace of the gospel of Jesus Christ. Therefore, my brothers and sisters, having an affinity of spirit with Minister Farrakhan is biblically incorrect. To cooperate with a spirit that is against the revelation of Jesus Christ is to operate against Christ.

There are some reverends who are leaving the church to embrace other religions, denying the deity of Christ and agreeing with other spirits. As Rev. Taylor stated in *The Final Call* newspaper, "I find an affinity with your spirit," referring to the spirit of Minister Louis Farrakhan. The Bible warns us about the dangers of having an affinity of spirit with others who are not in agreement with God's Word.

An example of this is found in the Old Testament when Jehoshaphat was the king of Judah. He followed the example of his father's early years. He did not worship idols, unlike King Ahab of Israel, who abandoned the God of Israel and began to worship foreign gods. However, the day came when Jehoshaphat thought it would be politically convenient to cooperate with unholy King Ahab to accomplish his purposes.

> Now Jehoshaphat had riches and honor in abundance, and joined *affinity* with Ahab.
>
> —2 Chronicles 18:1 KJV, emphasis added

In the Hebrew, the definition of the word affinity comes from a primitive root meaning: to give away in marriage, to contract affinity by marriage, to join together. The English definition of affinity is a natural liking, relationship, or kinship. The problem with King Jehoshaphat is that he became unequally yoked (joined) with King Ahab.

So Ahab, king of Israel, said to Jehoshaphat, king of Judah,

> "Will you go with me against Ramoth Gilead?" And he answered him, "I am as you are, and my people as your people; we will be with you in the war."
>
> —2 Chronicles 18:3 NKJV

They made their plans for war first, and later, as a formality, inquired of the Lord. Sound familiar? But God had a faithful prophet on hand, despised as he was by King Jehoshaphat because he always told the truth.

> And Jehu the son of Hanani the seer went out to meet him, and said to King Jehoshaphat, "Should you help the wicked and love those who hate the LORD? Therefore the wrath of the LORD is upon you. Nevertheless good things are found in you, in that you have removed the wooden images from the land, and have prepared your heart to seek God.
>
> —2 Chronicles 19:2-3 NKJV

They ignored the prophet and threw him into prison, then sent him to war. Ahab died in battle, and Jehoshaphat barely escaped with his life. He repented, but it didn't last long. Apparently he also joined forces with another evil king.

After this Jehoshaphat, king of Judah, allied himself with Ahaziah, king of Israel, who acted very wickedly. And he allied himself with him to make ships to go to

Tarshish, and they made the ships in Ezion Geber. But Eliezer, the son of Dodavah of Mareshah, prophesied against Jehoshaphat.

> "Because you have allied yourself with Ahaziah, the LORD has destroyed your works." Then the ships were wrecked, so that they were not able to go to Tarshish.
> —2 Chronicles 20:35-37 NKJV

The same is true today; we cannot be joined in a spiritual purpose with unbelievers and call it wholesome. It is, in reality, an unholy and unwise alliance that always brings serious consequences.

God Made from One Blood Every Nation

God does not have a problem with color. The separation of the nations by God was according to three things: language, families, and nation. Race, the color of one's skin, has *never* been a basis of separation (Genesis 10:1-5). According to Genesis, Noah had three sons—Shem, Ham, and Japheth. From them seventy nations were birthed. Twenty-six nations came from the line of Shem. Thirty nations came from Ham and fourteen from Japheth. The number seventy represents nations. Jesus sent out seventy disciples representing the nations (Luke 10:1), and there were seventy members of the Sanhedrin court. The genetic makeup of all nations was contained within these three men.

However, nations are no longer being formed. Everyone who exists now is part of a nation that existed then.

> He created all people of the world from one man, Adam, and scattered the nations across the face of the earth. He decided beforehand which should rise, and fall, and

when. He determined their boundaries. His purpose in all of this is that they should seek after him and find him, though he is not far from any one of us.

—Acts 17:26-27 TLB

Here is the lineage of Shem, Ham, and Japheth:

Ancestral Line	**Nation**	**Note**
Japheth (Genesis 10:2)	Greeks (Europeans)	(Became known as Gentiles)
Gomer (Genesis 10:2)	Russians, Germans	
Magog (Genesis 10:2)	Scythians	
Madai (Genesis 10:2)	Medes	
Javan (Genesis 10:2)	Greeks	
Tubal (Genesis 10:2)	Iberians	
Meshech (1 Chronicles 1:5)	Muscovites	
Tiras (1 Chronicles 1:5)	Thracians	
Ashkenaz (Genesis 10:3)	Germans	
Togarmah (Genesis 10:3)	Armenians, Turks	
Elishah (Genesis 10:3)	Hellenists	All of Greece
Tarshish (Genesis 10:4)	Spanish	
Kittim (Genesis 10:4)	Cyprus	

Ancestral Line	**Nation**	**Note**
Ham (Genesis 10:6)		
Cush (Genesis 10:6)	Ethiopia	
Mizraim (Genesis 10:6)	Egyptians	
Put (Phut or Punt) (Genesis10:6)	Libya	
Canaan (Genesis 10:6)	Canaanites	Only one of Ham's sons without a homeland
Seba (Genesis 10:7)	Sudan (Sabeans)	
Heth (Genesis 10:15)	Hittites	
Sin'Sidon' (Genesis 10:15)	China	"Sinology"
Ham	American Indian, Mongoloids	

Ancestral Line	**Nation**	**Note**
Shem	Jews	Genesis 10:21
Elam	Elamites	
Asshur	Assyrians	
Lud	Lydians	
Arphaxad	Chaldeans	
Aram	Arameans	Aramaic language

God has given to every nation (Shem, Ham, Japheth) an appointed time and boundaries for their habitation. There was an appointed time for each nation (Shem, Ham, Japheth) to reign and rule. However, at the end of each nation's reign there was disaster and chaos. Ham's ancestral reign lasted for two thousand years and was followed by the reign of Shem (Semitic line) for another two thousand years. We are now in the reign of Japheth (Japhethic line). The world is now in a state of chaos and confusion, which again points to the end of another reign. The reign of these brothers was not the answer to man's dilemma. We are at the end of our human strength. The next reign to come is that of the kingdom of God.

> Then the seventh angel sounded: And there were loud voices in heaven, saying, "The Kingdoms of this world have become the kingdom of our Lord and His Christ, and He shall reign forever and ever!
>
> —Revelation 11:15 NKJV

Continuing Dialogue

I wanted to include some significant testimonies I have gleaned over the years as well as the responses I have received to sharing my own testimony. In these responses you will hear people relating to my story, people struggling with their own circumstances and questions, and others who are angry and very defensive. It is important that Christians and Muslims continue to find the courage to dialogue in all honesty and integrity. The following are e-mails sent in response to my testimony, which is posted on the Internet at www.answering-islam.org.[23] I have left names out for privacy and the protection of converts.

12/29/00 South Africa, Pretoria: *I was really knocked over by your testimony. I was born and bred in a Muslim community in South Africa, Pretoria. I would like to know more about how you have dealt with the change back to Christianity. The trinity* *has always been a stumbling block for Muslims. I too sometimes find myself confused. So many Christians speak of God as being three different persons, instead of three manifestations of personality. I am twenty-four years old and gave my heart to Jesus one and a half years ago. It is so encouraging to see Muslims becoming Christians, especially you, because you were a leader in Islam. Yours in Christ, R.*

R's testimony:

I was born Muslim and grew up in a Muslim community. Islam was a way of life, a routine I never questioned, only passively accepted. About three years before I met Jesus I started becoming very "religious." I prayed my daily prayer and started to fast as is required of Muslims. I desired to know God more, but the deeper I delved into Islam the more my thirst grew. Being a female, I felt very trapped since I was not allowed to go to the mosque daily like the men, amongst many other prohibitions that exist regarding Muslim women. My thirst was not quenched and my experience in God was not being fulfilled. However, I remained content being who I was because I did not know anything better. Then one day a friend invited me to Rhema. I had been to Catholic Mass before and knew about Jesus so I expected things to be the same. However, this day was different. From the moment we drove through the gates I was taken in. Pastor Ray preached about how God called Moses, which really got my attention because as a Muslim I too believed in Moses. I experienced a whirlwind of emotions and gave my heart to Jesus even though I had no idea what I was doing. The next morning I became sick at work and my boss told me to go to the doctor. I walked all over town but could not find one without an appointment. As I walked around I eventually found myself standing before a Christian bookstore that I had never seen before—even though I had been working in that area for four years. Hesitantly, I stepped inside and immediately my eyes fell upon a bright yellow book with an Arabic cover. Needless to say, it got my attention. I walked out of the store having purchased a Bible as well as the book, which turned out to be a guide to Muslims on Christianity. All praise be to God forever because I managed to read the Gospel of Matthew while I was on sick leave and my life has never been the same since! God's Word struck deep chords within my spirit; turn the other cheek instead of an eye for eye (which is what Muslims still believe). As I read the Gospel more and more I realized that this is where God is. It became an indisputable fact to my heart and mind and I have been living for him ever since. Even though I experienced pain and rejection from those closest to me, I have found liberty, peace, and love that only Jesus can bring. He is the Ancient of days. The same God, yesterday, today, and forever, the great "I Am" that Moses spoke about. He is the only True God!

11/16/99 Egypt, Delta Region: *For the sake of security I go by the name T. I too am a former Muslim. I am being persecuted for my conversion to Christianity. Please pray for me. In Christ your brother T.*

05/02/01 Kenya, Africa: *I have read your testimony. It brought tears to my eyes. Would you help me with some questions? Peace be with you. Nun Sis.*

10/26/02: *I am a white Christian man who has been struggling with the appeal Islam has for African Americans. Your testimony leads me to believe that it is intolerance, bigotry, fear, and racism on the part of white Americans that appears to drive people like yourself into Islam, which appears, initially, to be a tolerant, friendly, accepting way of life. I praise God for your story and pray for your continued safety and strength as* *you go forward in a difficult but God-pleasing direction. Your friend in Christ R.*

01/10/01: *Sir, my name is J. ... I was very moved by your story. I recently was married. My wife has been raised a Baptist. I was raised as a Catholic. I was saved back in 1993. My wife recently had lunch with a few friends and a man who started telling her Islam was the true religion. I believe she is a little confused about some things that the Bible says. She has mentioned that she would like to become a Muslim. I have very strong reservations about that. I am wondering if you could shed some light on how I can explain to her Jesus died for her and that He was conceived miraculously. I was once told that there was a verse in the Qur'an that basically proves that Jesus is the Son of God. Any help in this matter would be greatly appreciated. May the Lord bless you.*

E-mail from Saudi Arabia: *I was born in Saudi Arabia as a member of a Muslim family. We were a very happy family, and I loved my relationship with them. I also felt very happy because I did all the things that God asked me to. I learned one sixth of the Quran by heart and a lot from the Hadith. When I was a teenager, I was an imam in the mosque. I fasted during the month of Ramadan, and prayed five times a day or more and even made Hajj. I had a desire to meet God at the last day, even when I had no guarantee. But I always hope for this. My hope grew when I started to think about fighting in the name of God (Jihad) in Afghanistan. I was sixteen years old. My parents would not let me go because I was too young. I always had love and respect for the Muslim people. There was no love or respect in my heart for the Christians, and the Jews were my first enemy. ...After some time, the devil found his way into our home and our life, and my life became very hard. Slowly, I drifted far away from God until the time that I believed in no*

God at all. My life became so busy. I had a very good job and earned a lot of money. Still I was not happy because I was afraid for the day that I would die. Sometimes a question would come to my mind—will I be with God in heaven or not? And it was very frightening to think about this, even for seconds. What about my future? One day I had a big problem in my life. I was in my room looking through the window up to the sky. Then I remembered God, and I wanted to pray to him to ask him for help, but which God should I pray to, Allah? I was sure that he was very angry with me because I had not prayed for a very long time. Or Jesus? I knew he had done a lot of miracles in the lives of other people. Then I said. "Jesus, help me!" I do not know why I spoke like this. I sat down on my bed and spoke to myself, "What is this stupid thing you just did?" Anyway, I did not expect anything to happen or the problem to go away. However, one and a half days later, my problem was solved! I decided to find out who this Jesus is. Is he God as the Christian people say, or is he a prophet, as I know from Islam? On the third day, that night I had a dream. I was standing in a cross shape with a low wall around it. In my right hand, I had a big stack of white unwritten papers. I was standing at the cross beam, and I was looking to a small group of people who were standing at the top. They all wore long white clothing, but one of them was different. He was standing at the right side, and with his left hand, he was leading the people through a door in the wall. Beyond the door was light, and I could not see what was in there. One moment I was standing in the dream, and the next moment I was seeing the cross from above. It was difficult for me to understand this. When I woke the next morning, I felt a very beautiful happiness in my heart that I never had before. And I felt a love in my heart and from inside my body a very special feeling. I felt also I just wanted to walk and to walk and ask everyone I met, do you know Jesus? It was more than a great feeling. It was a happiness that I've never known before in my life.

04/19/01 Decatur, Alabama: *Hi, my name is X; I live in Decatur, Alabama. I have a really good friend who is involved with the Nation of Islam (NOI). I read your article on the Internet and figured that if anyone could help me, you could. I am not asking for you to travel out here or anything, but maybe you can send my friend a letter or e-mail. He is smart, and I would hate to see him go to hell for something as deceptive as the teaching of the NOI. Please help.*

08/23/01: *I am considering Islam; in fact, I have taken Shahada (faith declaration). I was a Christian but I always felt like I was struggling. I always felt like God did not hear my prayers, or like I was in a deep forest. How do you explain the peace of mind I have when I read the Quran or hadiths? If this is not from God, then whom am I receiving these revelations from? As you may gather, this is very serious and I need objective advice. I am open to the fact that it can be wrong, but I need your help.*

01/20/02: *Brother, I read your article and honesty from the beginning of your story. I was getting interested on how tremendously you were being developed to the side of Islam. However, I am disappointed to say, as you went on with your article, you started to state such false, negative, unheard comments about the religion of Islam. I apologize if I sound un-polite but I have to say, such games or criticism towards any religion is childish, and stupidity. I have to say, you have done a great work on detailing everything on your article but not so great on convincing or even making any reader believe about your whole point; whatever that might be. Anyway, it is certainly not surprising to find such hate and jealousy towards Islam. I mean it is the number one growing religion in the world. Despite all the hate and jealousy some people or religions might have towards Islam, you and I and the world know that the hate-suppression that is practiced on Islam by others will not stop Islam into growing larger percentages than Christianity, Judaism, Catholic, each year. Since September 11, there have been twenty thousand converters to Islam. Anyway, as I was saying, stop this jealousy and phony facts that you say about Islam or any degree of criticism or insults towards the religion of peace and of course, it is the religion for white, black, yellow, brown, red, and all people.*

03/28/02: *I just wanted to tell you how blessed I was for being able to read your testimony. And I thank God for that. Although many of the events happened before my time, I was truly blessed! I just recently accepted Jesus Christ as my savior last January 2001 and have been in love with the Lord ever since. Your testimony was a true source of encouragement when I read it on the Internet. My biological dad and I have never really had a truly good and healthy relationship, but he has always claimed the teaching found in the Quran and to be a Muslim (part-time). I have been praying for his salvation and that he comes to know the Lord. Your testimony has given me an even greater insight on just what to pray for. I thank you for your obedience and courage. May God continue to richly bless you and your family!*

11/28/07 Houston, Texas: *I just read your testimony and I was blessed by it. I am printing it and sending it to my cousin who has been incarcerated in prison for the past fifteen years. He just became a Muslim and I am sending him some powerful testimonies. Please pray that his heart is open to receive Christ. God bless you and thank you for writing your testimony. May you bear much fruit for the kingdom of God. In Christ R*

01/12/08: *I read your letter on how you were in the Nation of Islam (NOI), and would like to know if you have any advice for me. My friend is on his way to prison and he believes everything Farrakhan has to say. I pray that more ex-NOI would speak up like you, my brother in Christ. Could you explain something or reveal some fallacies in the doctrine of the NOI. Thank you again for your testimony. God bless, D*

04/09/08: *Subject: I pity you, dear brother, it is either you were a fake and just made up this story of your conversion or you are real and you really experienced what you wrote. I truly feel sorry for you. You have embraced Islam and then let it go. After reading the story, I could only guess that your mistake is when you challenge Allah (God) on proving which religion is the right one. First, a true believer of Islam will never challenge Allah (God) because it is a display of arrogance in front of the Almighty. Second, if you were a true believer, you would not be so secure about your own degree of faith and always try to nurture it because it is not a static state, but always fluctuates. Finally, if you were already sure about Islam, why take the challenge at all? There is no point in it but to expose yourself to arrogance. Just because of your lack of knowledge, then you were trapped by your twin sister and yourself. I pity you. From a Muslim woman living in the U.S.*

One of the most well-known Islamic conversion stories involves a former professor of Islamic history at Al-Azhar University. His name is Mark A. Gabriel (not his birth name). He was also an imam of a mosque in Giza, Egypt. You can read about his testimony online by searching testimony of Mark Gabriel. He has authored many good books regarding his conversion and shares a unique perspective on the way Christians can best relate to those who hold to the teachings of Islam. He writes from his experience:

Presenting the gospel to Muslims has been famously difficult. One overlooked factor is that many Muslims believe they have been horribly wronged by Christians. The Muslim psyche is steeped with the history of conflicts between Muslims and those perceived to be Christians or representatives of the church. Though Muslims generally started the conflicts, today's Muslims ignore this fact and remember only their own offenses.

For example, Muhammad ordered his army to attack the Byzantine Christian army of more than 80,000, but Muslims remember only how 7,000 Muslim soldiers were slaughtered and just 3,000 returned home. Later, Muhammad's successors continued to fight against the Byzantine Empire until they captured Turkey and converted the majestic Ayasofia Cathedral into a mosque.

Muslims seethe over stories about Crusaders from the West who came and conquered Jerusalem in 1099, riding their horses through Al-Aqsa Mosque, where the blood of thousands of Muslims covered the horses' hooves. They bitterly remember the disaster of 1918 when British General Sir Edmund Allenby declared victory over Palestine and brought about the end of the Ottoman Empire, which had united and ruled the Muslim world for more than 600 years.

Americans may say: "That is in the past. We have to move on." That might be true from the American point of view, but in the Muslim culture, an offense against a Muslim in the past is like an offense against all Muslims today. As a result, Muslim ears are closed to the gospel message because of their anger about actions of those perceived to be Christians.

We must humble ourselves and confess the sins of our past. We need to tell Muslims: "We confess that Christians have sinned against you. We will not defend or excuse what was done. The Crusaders and those like them have violated the teachings of Jesus. We ask your forgiveness for what they did. We covenant to honor and respect the Muslim community in every way." These words need to be said one-on-one and on public platforms every chance we have.

A person who knows history may respond: "These apologies are unnecessary. What about the atrocities that Muslims have committed against Christians? The Muslims threatened the West first, and the Crusades were a response."

This is all true. Yet the response from Christians was not always Christlike. What did Jesus teach in the Lord's Prayer? "Forgive us our sins as we forgive those who sin against us" (see Matt. 6:14-15, Mark 11:25, Luke 6:37). As the church forgives Muslims for their sins against us, the church must also repent for the actions of Christians.

For example, the churches in Muslim countries have suffered so much that many of them have abandoned evangelism. Or, in an effort to make peace, some Eastern churches try to blur the lines between Christianity and Islam.

On the other hand, in the West I have noticed an interesting phenomenon. Conservative Christians love to hear my testimony and how I was persecuted by Muslims. My story helps them to reinforce their beliefs about the danger of Islam. But often these Christians are not looking for ways to help Muslims know about the truth.

In contrast, liberal Christians seem to think, "Maybe Muslims are worshiping the same God we are and

> everything will be OK if we just leave them alone." If the church knew anything about Allah, the God of the Quran, they would know that he and the God of the Bible could never be the same.
>
> Both attitudes in the Western church produce the same result: weak support for Muslim outreach. How I pray the Holy Spirit's conviction will be felt by every believer in Jesus and that the love of Jesus will begin to flow through them to the entire Muslim world.[24]

Praise be to God, the power of the gospel is still changing lives.

> Ask, and it will be given to you; seek, and you will find; knock, and it will be opened to you. For everyone who asks receives, and he who seeks finds, and to him who knocks it will be opened. Or what man is there among you who, if his son asks for bread, will give him a stone? Or if he asks for a fish, will he give him a serpent? If you then, being evil, know how to give good gifts to your children, how much more will your Father who is in heaven give good things to those who ask Him! Therefore, whatever you want men to do to you, do also to them, for this is the Law and the Prophets.
>
> —Matthew 7:7-12 NKJV

Local Resources

THE TABERNACLE OF Glory Church in Asbury Park, New Jersey, offers Reaching Muslims Ministry Workshops and Teaching on:

- Orthodox Islam
- Nation of Islam
- Five Percenters

Church phone (732) 774-8353
Church e-mail: TabofGlory@aol.com
Church Web site: www.TabofGlory.org

The Rev. Alexis Johnson (formerly known as Khalif Majid Hassan) is available for speaking engagements:

Mailing Address: P.O. Box 654
Asbury Park, NJ 07712
Personal e-mail: alxakj@aol.com

Additional copies of this book are available by contacting:

- Minister Johnson
- Pleasant Word Publishing, 1730 Railroad St., Enumclaw, WA 98022, phone: (800) 326-4674
- Winepress Publishing Group at (877) 421-7323 or www.winepressbooks.com
- Your local Christian bookstore
- Online at Amazon.com, BarnesandNoble.com, and ChristianBooks.com

Reverend Alexis Johnson has been in prison ministry for more than twelve years and is in the process of raising funds to provide transitional housing for the inmates of the Monmouth County Correctional Institution in Freehold, New Jersey.

Author's Notes

Chapter One: My Black Experience

† My parents moved to Red Bank in 1941. As of this writing, my mother is ninety years old and still has a good memory. She was able to tell me what the racial atmosphere was like in Red Bank during the early 1940s.

‡ In 1923, Red Bank Mayor William H. R. White was overruled by the borough council in his attempt to deny the Klan a permit to march.

* Amelia married Joseph in 1986. Joseph now serves Christ as pastor of a church in Asbury Park, New Jersey.

+ One of the most well-known Muslim conversion stories involves a former professor of Islamic history at Al-Azhar University who was also an imam of a mosque in Giza, Egypt. His name is Mark A. Gabriel (not his birth name) and you can find his testimony all over the Internet and on YouTube.com. He has also written several informative books and articles for Christian publishers.

Chapter Two: History of a Counterfeit Nation

† This is exactly what I was taught: Fard Muhammad's father had lain with a white woman he called a devil, and she became pregnant. Fard Muhammad taught that his father married this woman and that the first child she birth for him was a girl, and his father said, "Uhm, I missed that time!" So he tried again and the result was a son, Fard Muhammad. Fard said his father took special care of him so that he might be sent among the Western people, the Caucasian people, or by their real name, "the devils." He needed one of these devil people in order to complete his purpose. Elijah Muhammad said that he was taught by Fard Muhammad that his father was a black man and that his father knew Fard could not be successful in coming to a solid white country as a solid black man. Therefore, Fard's father said, "I will go and make a son. And I will send my son among them, looking like them. They will think my son is one of them, and he will find our lost people." This is the "God in the flesh" of the Nation of Islam. Fard Muhammad taught that his father left the Holy City of Mecca, found a blond-haired white woman from the hills of Asia, brought her back and cleaned her of her own evil. The evil tendencies of the woman and the very spirit of evil was taken from her; and she was made by him a perfect, holy, and righteous woman. Perhaps Fard Muhammad is alluding to a type of "immaculate conception" in justification of his white mother.

‡ Warith Deen Muhammad continued as one of the most influential African-American Muslim leaders until his death on September 9, 2008, of heart disease and complications from diabetes. He died at his home in Illinois, a little more than a week after giving his last sermon wherein he repeatedly praised Jesus and Muhammad as great leaders. Over the course of his ministry, he had repeatedly called for the cooperation of both faiths.

Endnotes

Chapter One: My Black Experience

1. Randall Gabrielan, *Images of America–Red Bank*. Dover, NH. Arcadia Publishing, 1995. 82.
2. Alex Haley, Malcolm X, *The Autobiography of Malcolm X*, New York, NY. 1964. 305.
3. Black Apologetics Ministry Web site, http://www.blackapologetics.com/index.html ; http://www.blackapologetics.com/fivepercentfaq.html, August 14, 2008.
4. Black Apologetics Ministry Web site, http://www.blackapologetics.com/index.html; http://www.blackapologetics.com/fivepercentbeliefs.html, August 14, 2008.
5. Black Apologetics Ministry Web site, http://www.blackapologetics.com/index.; http://www.blackapologetics.com/fivepercentfaq.html, August 14, 2008.

Chapter Two: History of a Counterfeit Nation

6. This information comes from what I learned while I was with the organization with some gleanings from the book *Message To The Blackman In America* by Elijah Muhammad, Muhammad Temple of Islam Publishing Company, Phoenix, AZ. 1965.

7. Toure Muhammad. *Chronology of Nation of Islam History*, Honorable Elijah Muhammad Educational Foundation, Chicago, IL. 1996.

8. *The Final Call*, October 19, 1999, page 17.

9. *The Final Call*, December 14, 1994.

10. *The Final Call*, December 14, 1994

11. Hunter-Gault, Charlayne. "PBS Online Newshour–Million Man March." *Public Broadcasting System*. 16 Oct. 1995. PBS. 4 Sept. 2008 <http://www.pbs.org/newshour/bb/race_relations/race_relations_10-16a.html>. Transcript of News Report.

12. "CNN–U.S. News–Minister Farrakhan Challenges Black Men." *CNN–Cable News Network*. 17 Oct. 1995. CNN–Cable News Network, Inc. 4 Sept. 2008 <http://www.cnn.com/US/9510/megamarch/10-16/transcript/index.html>. Transcript of News Report.

13. Ibid.

14. *The International Islamic Conference*, July 6, 1997, Chicago, Illinois, McCormick Center, Grand Auditorium – VHS Video Produced by NOI.

Chapter Three: My Message to the Churches

15. Edgerly, Adam, Ellis, Carl. *Emergence of Islam in the African American Community, Reach Out*. Answering-

Islam.org. 22 Jan. 2009 <http://www.answering-islam.org/ReachOut/>.

16. Muhammad, James. *The Final Call*, June 30, 1993, page 9.
17. Muhammad, James. *The Final Call*, June 30, 1993, page 9.
18. Muhammad, James. *The Final Call*, June 30, 1993, page 9.
19. What The Muslims Believe; *The Final Call*, last page.
20. What The Muslims Believe; The Final Call, last page.
21. What The Muslims Believe; The Final Call, last page.
22. What The Muslims Believe; The Final Call, last page.
23. http://www.answering-islam.org/Testimonies/hassan.html.

Continuing Dialogue

24. Reprinted with permission from *Charisma & Christian Life*, 2005. Copyright Strang Communications Co., USA. All rights reserved. www.charismamag.com.